WHY DO JEWISH?

A MANIFESTO FOR 21ST CENTURY JEWISH PEOPLEHOOD

ZACK BODNER

gefen
publishing house בית תרצאות לאור
JERUSALEM ◆ NEW YORK
Est. 1981

Cover Design: James Bailey
Cover illustration: James Bailey
Typesetting: Estie Dishon

ISBN: 978-965-7801-05-5

2 4 6 8 9 7 5 3

Gefen Publishing House Ltd.
6 Hatzvi Street
Jerusalem 9438614,
Israel
972-2-538-0247
orders@gefenpublishing.com

Gefen Books
c/o Baker & Taylor Publisher Services
30 Amberwood Parkway
Ashland, Ohio 44805
516-593-1234
orders@gefenpublishing.com

www.gefenpublishing.com

Printed in Israel
Library of Congress Control Number: 2021909741

TACHLIS (tókh-liss) *n.* Yiddish, textual Hebrew.

1. Practical details, "brass tacks" (as in, "Stop talking already and let's get down to brass tacks. Let's talk *tachlis!*")

2. Heart of a matter, underlying purpose (as in, "Nu? *Tachlis!* What's the point you're trying to make!?")

3. A model for reimagining Jewish Peoplehood for the twenty-first century based on doing Jewish, framed as an acronym:

> T – Tikkun Olam
>
> A – Art and Culture
>
> C – Community
>
> H – Holidays and Rituals
>
> L – Learning
>
> I – Israel
>
> S – Shabbat and Spirituality

Advance Praise

"Why Do Jewish is a reflective and prophetic, engaging and insightful, delightful and important book. Zack Bodner writes from his perch in the Silicon Valley where he is eye-witness to the tectonic changes that will shape what he perceptively calls Jewish Peoplehood 4.0. In a winning combination of personal anecdote and observation, he reviews from whence we came, spotlights where we are, and posits important questions that both individuals and institutions must answer as we craft the Jewish future. A must read for leaders of all Jewish organizations who seek to engage the next generation of entrepreneurial, creative, and DIY Jewish influencers."

> —Dr. Ron Wolfson, Fingerhut Professor of Education at American Jewish University, author of *Relational Judaism: Using the Power of Relationships to Transform the Jewish Community*

"A great read and a very important contribution to the discussion on how to ensure the continued significant renaissance of the Jewish People. The Jewish People will not BE if the Jewish Person does not DO. This message coming from someone so rooted in the Jewish Community Center Movement is a much-needed breath of fresh air. Thank you, Zack."

> —Avraham Infeld, President Emeritus at Hillel International, author of *A Passion for A People*

"Zack Bodner has done that rare thing — written a book that makes those who of us who love being Jewish want to revisit the tradition anew, and those who have written off Judaism want to take a second look. *Why Do Jewish* explains our magical inheritance in concrete, accessible, relevant terms, and gives us a roadmap to explore it, understand it, practice it, and pass it on. Add this book to your personal library and recommend it to those whom you know are searching for meaning and what matters.

> —Abigail Pogrebin, author of *My Jewish Year: 18 Holidays, One Wondering Jew*

"Bodner offers a personal and heartfelt call for an active, vibrant and meaning-filled Judaism in the contemporary era. His focus on the lived experiences of Jews, in the United States, Israel, and throughout history, testifies to the dynamic nature of Judaism and the possibilities that Jewish peoplehood offers. In Bodner's book we read a manifesto for twenty-first century Jewish life."

> —Professor Marc Dollinger, Goldman Chair in Jewish Studies and Social Responsibility at San Francisco State University, author of *Black Power, Jewish Politics: Reinventing the Alliance in the 1960s*

"Zack Bodner has written an important manifesto for our times. I liked it when I agreed with it – and loved it when I disagreed with it. His level-headed, deep-hearted, thoughtful and thought-provoking ideas about why be Jewish and how to do Jewish in the twenty-first century are just the right spur for the kind of debate we need about who we are – and what we must become."

> —Professor Gil Troy, author of *The Zionist Ideas* and *Why I Am a Zionist*

"Zack Bodner brings to all his work – on behalf of Israel, American Jewish communities, now, his writing – both an infectious love for Judaism and the Jewish people as well as a deep intelligence. His passion, his wit and his devotion to life rich with meaning make this book a wonderful read."

—Daniel Gordis, Shalem College in Jerusalem, author of *Israel: A Concise History of a Nation Reborn*.

"Since the Shoah, the Jewish world has been understandably focused, somehow, on ensuring the survival of our people. Now that continuity appears increasingly firm, at least for a while, more and more of us, around the world, allow ourselves to yearn for what lies beyond the existential objectives that have occupied our families for generations. *Why Do Jewish* is an important map to that more enlivened future. Excitingly, Zack Bodner locates some of the waypoints to this future in our distant past, weaving tradition, hands-on ideas, and a fearless sense of what is and should be possible for the Jewish people."

—Michael Fertik, NYT Bestselling Author & Jewish Philanthropist

"This is a work grounded in research, but also highly accessible. With the spirit of an explorer, Bodner examines foundational questions around Judaism, anchoring his study in real world examples drawn from a lifetime of working across Jewish experiences. His open-minded approach offers a lively, readable guide to anyone looking to re-examine how they "do Jewish.""

—Anne Kornblut, Pulitzer Prize winning journalist

"Fusing personal reflections with the sophisticated wisdom of SIlicon Valley, Zack Bodner charts the future application for the 5,000 years old "operating system" of Judaism. This thoughtful book offers a compelling case for the critically called for leaps ahead, towards the co-creation of a better balanced, bold and brave new era for global Jewish life."

—Rabbi Amichai Lau Lavie

"In Why Do Jewish?, Zack Bodner offers a compelling roadmap for the future of Jewish life. By sharing personal stories and deep insights from Judaism's greatest thinkers, he answers the burning question of how the Jewish people can thrive in the modern world. This book is a must-read for anyone looking for how to live a meaningful life with Jewish values as their guide."

—Saul Singer, co-author of Start-Up Nation: The Story of Israel's Economic Miracle

"Judaism isn't a spectator's sport. In a friendly down-to-earth passionate tone, with humor and depth, Bodner is giving fresh answers to the ancient questions Jews have been always asking: why, how, and what makes them Jews. COVID-19 is an equalizer, that made us all stop for the past year and rethink why, what, and how to live the years ahead. Zack Bodner wrote the book that gives cutting-edge answers. I read it with delight and was left full of hope."

—Ruth Calderon, Founder and Director of Alma Home for Hebrew Culture, author of A Bride for One Night: Talmud Tales

"Zack Bodner's *Why Do Jewish* speaks to this moment with humor, kindness, eloquence, and honesty – precisely the ingredients necessary if we are to build a Judaism that is meaningful, relevant, and joyous. In this thoughtful exploration of Jewish identity and tradition, you will find an invitation to one passionate and loving writer's soul. But what's even more precious is that this *mentch* has made room for our curiosity and disagreement along the way, proving that this unprecedented Jewish moment - a strong Jewish homeland *and* a strong Jewish diaspora - is blessed with leaders whose hearts and minds are big enough for us all. It doesn't get more Jewish than that!"

—Rabbi Menachem Creditor, Scholar in Residence at UJA-Federation New York, editor of *When We Turned Within: Reflections on COVID-19 (Vols. 1 & 2)*

"Bodner poses the most relevant question in Judaism today, and he brings practical answers from the trenches of the fight for Jewish continuity. Bodner's insights will bring energy and perspective to an expanding and vital conversation between parents, educators and Jewish community leaders."

—Tal Keinan, Author of *God Is In the Crowd*

"*Why Do Jewish? A Manifesto for 21st Century Jewish Peoplehood* is brilliant and required reading for anyone who wants to explore why Jewish wisdom is so relevant and important for living a good life and building a good society."

—Tiffany Shlain, Emmy-nominated filmmaker, author of *24/6: The Power of Unplugging One Day a Week.*

"Writing from the front lines of the Jewish encounter with the 21st century, Zack Bodner offers a wise and courageous road map to navigating the challenges and opportunities of this time. With deep love for the Jewish people and its story, Bodner presents a vision of a Jewish community that embraces diversity and experimentation, even as it rediscovers the essentials of a timeless Jewish life. There is no better guide to the Jewish future than Zack Bodner; and as he makes clear in this compelling book, the future is now."

—Yossi Klein Halevi, Senior Fellow at Shalom Hartman Institute, author of *Letters to My Palestinian Neighbor*

"Zack Bodner is one of the most innovative leaders in today's American Jewish community, and this book is packed with ideas - about where we've come from, where we are headed, and what from our tradition can help us - in service of a vibrant Jewish future. Part study guide of the Jewish tradition, part handbook for creative leadership, this book should be an indispensable conversation piece for Jewish communal leaders in wrestling with our challenges and figuring out where to go."

—Dr. Yehuda Kurtzer, President of The Shalom Hartman Institute of North America

"*Why Do Jewish* is required reading for serious Jewish professionals and lay leaders thinking about the future of our people. Zack boldly explores the underlying challenges facing our community today and architects a meaningful, joyous and relevant operating system meant to sustain generations to come."

—Avi Jorisch, author of *Thou Shalt Innovate: How Israel Ingenuity Repairs the World*

"It's no surprise that a bold manifesto for rethinking the future of Judaism should come from the leader of the Jewish Community Center in the heart of Silicon Valley. I expect that each reader will agree with some of Zack Bodner's diagnoses and prescriptions and disagree with others, and Bodner would have it no other way. Bodner is asking the right questions, illustrated with compelling stories from his own efforts to live a meaningful Jewish life and from many years of Jewish communal leadership. *Why Do Jewish?* asks these tough questions openly and fearlessly, inviting readers to engage with the questions and vigorously debate the answers—and that is one Jewish tradition we can all agree must remain central no matter what the Jewish future brings."

—Dan Libenson, Co-host of the Judaism Unbound podcast

"Why Do Jewish is the book so many of us were waiting for. I am confident that it will become the main guidebook on how to practically connect Judaism to dynamic life in the 21st century."

—Micah Goodman, Israeli author

"Bringing together historical and sociological insight, text analysis and his vast personal experience in Jewish leadership, Zack Bodner offers a fresh response to the age-old question: "Why do Jewish?""

—Ruby Namdar, Author of *The Ruined House*

"Bodner's fresh and bold manifesto is a compelling synthesis of some of the most innovative ideas in the field, as well as his own insight and creativity, about how to reshape and revitalize the American Jewish community. This should be a must-read for any Jewish leader who seeks to make Jewish life and identity relevant and to bring them into alignment with today's worldview and zeitgeist."

—Rabbi Niles Goldstein, spiritual leader of Congregation Beth Shalom of Napa Valley, author of *Gonzo Judaism: A Bold Path for Renewing an Ancient Faith.*

"Words without deeds are nothing."
– David Ben-Gurion

"It is not our duty to finish the work,
But neither are we free to neglect it."
– Rabbi Tarfon, *Pirkei Avot* 2:16

Dedicated to my parents,

who taught me how to do Jewish,

to Ronit, for her unwavering patience, love, and support,

and to my children, Talia, Elie, and Orly,

who proudly carry the Jewish torch

into the future.

Contents

Acknowledgments

This book comes from twenty-five years of working, learning, and volunteering in the Jewish community. It comes from years of study and practice. It comes from years of personally searching. And it also comes from the love and guidance of family, friends, mentors, and many colleagues.

First, I want to thank my colleagues at the Oshman Family JCC. They have not only been thought partners for me on the theory behind this work, but they have been the ultimate practitioners as well. They are the true "Do Leaders" here, as they have put this theory into action, piloting, and prototyping many of the programs laid out here.

Sally Flinchbaugh, the COO of the JCC and my right hand, has been the person most responsible for the implementation of these innovative ideas at the JCC. Ronit Jacobs, Luba Palant, Tova Birnbaum, Amitai Fraiman, Zoe Jick, and the members of their teams have been instrumental in executing these ideas. They've also brought just as many of their own exciting and innovative ideas to the table, and I continue to aspire to create the right environment to allow them to dream big.

Nathaniel Bergson-Michaelson, the communication guru of the JCC, and his predecessor Mimi Sells, have helped put so many of my ambitious ideas into words. They've helped write and rewrite the catch-phrases, vision statements, and acronyms that cover the walls of the JCC and fill this book.

Seth Leslie, Mark Holtzman, and Sally Porush have also

been invaluable partners as we've explored what the future of Judaism could look like here at the JCC, while Carol Saal, Ric Rudman, Tali Ronen, Nicole Rubin, Susan Saal, Sharon Leslie, Daryl Messinger, and so many other JCC board leaders have been supportive of me and the staff as we've worked together to bring our collective vision into reality.

Avi Jorisch has been my dear friend and invaluable mentor along this writing journey. From the pep talks in the early days to the introduction to Ilan Greenfield at Gefen Publishing at a critical juncture along this path, I couldn't have made this book a reality with his help.

Rabbi Danny Gordis has been my rebbe, my advisor, and my friend since the beginning. From the many conversations over the years to the in-depth reading of an early draft of this book, his insights have been essential to my own growth as well as the creation of this project.

Doron Krakow has been my friend, colleague, and truth-teller on this book, as well as on all things Jewish. His comments and critiques of an early draft of this book were vital in making this a reality.

Ron Wolfson has also been an early advisor, motivator, and cheerleader throughout this project. He was the very first published author to read early drafts of this book and offer the much-needed encouragement to keep on keeping on.

Tad Taube has been incredibly generous with the OFJCC and with me personally for more than a decade. His support for this project in particular has been instrumental. I hope this book succeeds in furthering the important work at the heart of Taube Philanthropies' purpose, namely promoting the future of Jewish Peoplehood. Shana Penn, Executive Director of Taube Philanthropies, has been a supporter and editor of this project from the early days. She offered important insights and helped secure vital financial sponsorship for the publishing of this book.

Jeff Farber and Anita Friedman, as well as all my friends at the Koret Foundation, have been my most essential supporters from day one. In addition to their instrumental financial support for the OFJCC, they've continued to be advisors and friends to me personally through all the ups and downs.

Dan Libenson has been my partner in disrupting the Jewish establishment since his early days at *Judaism Unbound*. He was the first one to connect with me on the terminology of "Judaism 4.0," and has been key to introducing me to so many of the thought leaders architecting the Jewish future.

All my colleagues in the JCC movement nationally and globally, especially Mark Sokoll, Barak Hermann, Joel Dinkin, Joy Levitt, Lynn Wittels, Brian Schreiber, Jared Powers, Mark Shapiro, Brian Siegel, Michael Feinstein, Jonathan Lev, Henry Timms, Janet Elam, Todd Rockoff, Amy Lavin, Marci Glazer, Paul Geduldig, Lael Gray, Judy Wolf-Bolton, Melissa Chapman, Nate Stein, Jonathan Ornstein, Smadar Bar-Akiva, Nissan Gez, and so many others have been wonderful partners, colleagues, and companions through this journey.

Barry Finestone has been a confidant and friend from his very first days in San Francisco. Andrés Spokoiny has been an inspiring thought partner and articulate oracle along the way. Avraham Infeld has provided wisdom and clarity for me as I've formulated my thoughts around Jewish Peoplehood. Rabbi Niles Goldstein has been a good friend who's offered me essential encouragement and advice on the publishing world. And Shlomi Ravid, one of the earliest adopters of the language of Peoplehood, has inspired me for more than two decades on my own journey.

The Jewish LEAP Year is a reality because Nir Braudo and the leaders at BINA partnered with the OFJCC to make it so. Then, Kathy Fields Rayant and Garry Rayant were the very first ones to enthusiastically and generously support the LEAP Year vision and turn it into a reality. I owe them a tremendous debt of gratitude.

The Z3 Project exists today due to the foresight, tenacity, and generosity of the earliest supporters, including Orli and Zack Rinat, Katie and Amnon Rodan, the Paul E. Singer Foundation, the Seidel Family, Roselyne Swig, Laura and Gary Lauder, Eta and Sass Somekh, and Amy and Mort Friedkin. So many others joined in to help make Z3 a success over the years, including the Maimonides Fund, Our Common Destiny, the Fooksman Family Foundation, Eli and Jeanette Reinhard, Moses Libitzky, Yoram and Zehava Cedar, and so many others.

Elliot Brandt, Jon Missner, Elias Saratovsky, Brian Abrahams, Mike Sachs, Brian Shankman, Eric Geisser, Mark Kleinman, Matt Levin, Charlie Kirschner, Sarah Cohen, Dani Fisher, Jonathan Kessler, Rob Bassin, Richard Fishman, Howard Kohr, and all my friends at AIPAC taught me the importance of standing up for what matters, even if it isn't popular – especially when it comes to Israel. The AIPAC journey began thanks to my dear friend Sam Lauter and his mother, Naomi Lauter, of blessed memory.

Thought partners have been essential to my process over the years, and few have been as important as my friends at the Shalom Hartman Institute. From Yehuda Kurtzer to Rabbi Donniel Hartman, from Yossi Klein Halevi to Tal Becker, I've been blessed to swap ideas with some of the greatest Jewish thinkers living today.

My study partners have also pushed me to think differently and challenge my current way of looking at the world, including Rabbi Joey Felsen, Michael Fertik, and Zvi Weiss. Still others deserve immense appreciation for introducing me to authors who've opened new worlds for me, like Rabbi Lee Bycel who turned me on to Rabbi Abraham Joshua Heschel, Rabbi Darren Kleinberg who introduced me to Rabbi Yitz Greenberg, and Gidi Grinstein who introduced me to Rabbi Jonathan Sacks. These giants of Jewish wisdom have so enriched my life – thank you.

Of course this book would never have been published but for Ilan Greenfield and Gefen Publishing believing in me. I am grateful to Ilan for having confidence in me, to Daphne Abrahams for encouraging me, and to Renee Schwartz, my eagle-eyed editor, for her incredible attention to detail.

"The Yovel," my oldest friends from our time living and studying in Israel in 1994, taught me how to love life and seek adventure, while my friends in the Bay Area, born mostly from the JCC and Gideon Hausner Jewish Day School, taught me what it means to be a true community.

My Alcheck family taught me what it means to be supported unconditionally. They welcomed me into the family like I'd always been one of them, and introduced me to a new world of Sephardic traditions. (Who knew Sephardic charoset was so much better than the Ashkenazi version?) To Yael and Elie, Mike and Mallary, Riki and Bill, as well as Maury – thank you for always being the first ones to support me in everything I do.

My brother Gabe taught me the military ethos of

brotherhood and always being there for me no matter what. That's just what brothers do. Tamara, Noah, and Ethan showed me how to embrace change. Ellen and the Millstein crew taught me how to have a good time, even while fasting, and to make a few bets along the way.

My mother, Myrna, taught me what it means for a parent to love a child completely, and she always told me that things happen for a reason, which was my first notion that there might be a Divine plan. Thank you, Mom. I love you. My father, Paul, of blessed memory, taught me to follow my heart, embrace the journey, and always turn lemons into lemonade. Thank you, Dad. I miss you every day.

My kids, Talia, Elie, and Orly, teach me every day the importance of patience, laughter, acceptance, and grace. Talia reminds me how important it is to smile, be vulnerable, and show your soul to the world. Elie reminds me to be curious, ask questions, and never accept the status quo. And Orly reminds me to laugh, hug, dance, and embrace my creative spirit. I love you all more than you'll ever know.

Finally, my wife Ronit teaches me every day what true partnership is all about. She is my confidant, my consigliere, my therapist, my muse, and my number one fan. But most important, she is my best friend and *beshert*. This book only exists because she believed in me. I love you always, Ro.

Prologue

On December 21, 2014, my father passed away at sixty-eight. He had been diagnosed with stage four non-smoker's lung cancer two years prior, and the doctors had given him six months to live. My dad outlived their timeline by a factor of four, which we all believe was due to his remarkably positive attitude, his love of life, and his ability to turn lemons into lemonade.

My dad's moniker actually was "the Lemonade Man," and his motto – or in today's parlance, his "six-word memoir" – was: "Live with love, laughter, and lemonade." Not only could he always see the bright side of a situation, but he could often make it funny, too.

He had a wonderful sense of humor that spanned from ridiculous puns and silly dad jokes to expansive tall tales – and he had a laugh that could infect the whole room. Often, he was the first one to laugh at his own jokes, but it didn't matter because soon after, everyone else was joining in.

My dad truly thought laughter was the best medicine. In fact, during his cancer treatment, he was the one making all the nurses laugh. He loved to tell stories, and he'd often take tremendous artistic license in their retelling. Even after Google was invented, and the family would fact-check him and show that his stories were filled with half-truths, he'd stick to his guns and insist it happened like he said.

When it was time to eulogize my father, I ended up making

the theme of my remarks, "What my father taught me." Of course, in a short tribute, no one can capture everything they learned from a wonderful parent, but I did my best. Ultimately, I realized what my father really taught me was how to live a life of Jewish values, Jewish culture, Jewish stories, Jewish food, Jewish humor, Jewish rituals, Jewish history, Jewish holidays, Jewish ethics...basically, all the elements of Jewish Peoplehood.

But it wasn't a Jewish Peoplehood story that was static. It was incredibly dynamic, exciting, and often contradictory. For example, although he grew up in a kosher home, he didn't insist on our family having a kosher home. Instead, our home was what he called "kosher-style," meaning no *treif* in the house, but pepperoni pizza or moo-shoo pork at a restaurant were okay.[1]

One of my family's favorite memories of my father was when we all went out for a nice meal for his sixtieth birthday and he ordered the lobster bisque. We all looked at him quizzically, knowing he didn't eat shellfish, but without missing a beat, he asked the waiter to "hold the lobster." The waiter didn't understand and asked, "Sir? What do you mean? It's a lobster bisque." My father replied, "You know – the little lobster garnish on the top? You can leave that off."

In our family, we didn't keep Shabbat (the Sabbath) in the strictly traditional sense like my father did growing up, but we did have Shabbat dinner every Friday night where we lit candles, said blessings, drank Manischewitz wine, ate the traditional challah, and sang songs. When it came time for me to

---

1.   The term "kosher" refers to Jewish dietary laws and customs. *Treif* refers to items that are strictly forbidden for Jews to eat, including pork and shellfish.

attend my school dances on Friday nights, it was a wrestling match with my father because he felt that Friday nights were family nights and we should all be together for the evening. In the end, we found a compromise that allowed me to go to the school dances after our family Shabbat dinners – and my parents didn't even insist on coming with me as chaperones, though they did try.

We made our own rituals, too. Every Saturday morning, we'd go together to buy bagels, cream cheese, and lox from the local deli and we'd bring it home to share with the family. We didn't go to synagogue. We didn't pray. *That* was our Shabbos.[2]

Every Passover, after we'd have the traditional family Seder[3] and eat the big Passover meal complete with gefilte fish, chopped liver, brisket, and enough matzah to clog any healthy kid's plumbing, let alone an Ashkenazi kid with GI issues, my cousins and I would pass out watching *The Ten Commandments* – the one with Charlton Heston as Moses.

Every Hanukkah, my mom would make homemade latkes.[4] I remember the year my grandfather broke the garbage disposal by shoving the peels of three dozen potatoes down the sink hole. That story will forever be a part of Bodner family lore – and it has since led to us buying latkes rather than making them.

There was depth to the way our family lived Jewishly,

2. The Yiddish pronunciation for the word "Shabbat."
3. The Seder is the symbol-filled sharing of the story of the exodus of the Jews from Egypt, which Jews retell every year on Passover as part of a traditional annual meal.
4. Potato pancakes.

too. My parents often taught us lessons using Jewish values. I remember once when I was very young – I must have been four or five – we were at a restaurant and I saw an overweight man sitting nearby. According to my father, I announced quite loudly, so the entire restaurant could hear, "Dad, that's the fattest man I've ever seen!" Of course, my parents were mortified, but after slinking out of the restaurant, my father used it as a teaching moment, telling me that as Jews, we believe all human beings were made in the image of God. (You can imagine what I thought about God after that conversation.)

I also remember the time my older cousin Ralph drove to California from Maryland and just decided to stay in the Golden State – without any plan, any money, or any place to live. So my parents took him in, and Ralph ended up staying with us for months – even after he broke every rule in the house, including throwing a big party when my folks went out of town. Maybe this wasn't so much a lesson in "welcoming the stranger," since Ralph was family, but surely my parents demonstrated the Jewish value of audacious hospitality and extreme patience toward challenging guests!

Ultimately, my parents taught me how to live a meaningful life based on doing Jewish. Yes, you heard that right, I said "doing Jewish." My parents would have said "being Jewish" because that was the language we used in the late twentieth century. But what I now know is that we were really "doing Jewish" more than "being Jewish," and we were doing it in our own way.

Isn't that what Jews have done for centuries? Haven't the Jewish People evolved over the generations based on how we've assimilated into other societies?

What does the future look like? How will Jewish Peoplehood evolve over the next hundred years or more?

Clearly my experience growing up was very "Ashkenormative,"[5] but there are so many different types of Jews and hence, different Jewish experiences – how will they blend and merge together and change the Jewish future? The realization by the mainstream Jewish community that Mizrachi Jews, Jews of color, Asian Jews, and Indian Jews, for example, have stories that are vastly different but just as authentic will also impact the future.

And with more and more intermarriage, the Jewish story of the future will look much different than the past.

Now that there is a Jewish state once again, how will that impact the future of Jewish Peoplehood?

My hope is that however we evolve, we will do so in a way that ensures Jewish life remains meaningful, relevant, and joyful. Those are the three characteristics that Judaism must maintain or else risk becoming lost to many but its most traditional adherents.

Ultimately, however Judaism evolves, we must be able to answer that question that is so central for each generation: "Why be Jewish?" Or in this case, "Why do Jewish?"

This book is part manifesto for a new way of doing Jewish in the twenty-first century, for those Jews who are not traditionally observant, and part love letter to the Jewish People (and by extension, my full eulogy for my father). But it is

---

5.   A word used to describe an Ashkenazi-centric way of looking at the world. Ashkenazi Jews are those with roots in eastern Europe and Russia, as opposed to Sephardic Jews whose ancestors are from Spain, Turkey, Greece, the Middle East, and North Africa.

mostly my own answer to the question, "Why do Jewish?" It's been swimming around in my head for many years, and it's been worked through and worked over many times. So, it's about time it finally made its way onto paper – or a screen, or Audible, or in whatever version you're experiencing it.

I hope it gives you much to think about and much to disagree with. Mostly, I hope it inspires you to learn more about this three-thousand-year-old tradition that has given so much to me and my family. Hopefully, it can add meaning to your life as well.

So, pick up a glass of scotch, get cozy in your favorite reading chair, and crack open the book for a little read. Or if you're driving and listening to this, please forgo the scotch, for now.

L'chaim!

Introduction

When I was growing up in Claremont, California, a small suburb of Los Angeles, there weren't many Jews in my town. I was one of fewer than ten Jews in my whole graduating class – not even enough for a minyan.[1] Yet somehow, my two closest friends were Jewish.

One of them was from a South African family who took their Judaism seriously. They were not Orthodox, but came from a community in South Africa that was, so they engaged in practices that were respectful of Jewish tradition. For example, they honored Shabbat, even if they weren't fully Shabbat-observant; they observed the major holidays; they were very Zionistic; they had Judaica all over the house; and they talked about their Jewish identity frequently.

My other friend came from a very different family. Both his parents were second- or third-generation American Jews. They'd been assimilated for at least one full generation, and though they had their kids take off school for the High Holidays, they didn't observe much of the traditions. In fact, I

---

1. A minyan is a group of ten Jewish adults, the minimum number required by Jewish law to make a quorum. If you pray with less than ten, which is permitted, some prayers are said silently instead of aloud and other customs must also be left out of a prayer service.

remember one year my friend eating a ham and cheese sandwich on Yom Kippur after returning from synagogue![2]

I remember in high school, when my friend who ate the ham and cheese sandwich was seriously dating a non-Jewish girl, his father ripped into him, angry with his decision. I believe now, as I remember thinking then, that if his father cared so much, perhaps he should have helped his son better answer the question, why should he care about being Jewish?

This is the question at the heart of our quest. We must be able to answer that question for ourselves so we can answer it for our children and grandchildren. Why does being, or doing, Jewish matter? Why is it so important that we believe passing it on to future generations is vital? What does it have to say that can resonate so fully, that in each generation we make decisions where Jewish values, traditions, and ideas play a part? And above all, why are these questions so hard for so many today to answer?

I believe a combination of three core questions is making it hard to answer so many of those other questions: the "why," the "what" and the "how" we do Jewish.

First, many Jews today cannot answer the "why" because they do not find Judaism relevant in our modern age.[3] Some

---

2. Yom Kippur is a holiday when Jews traditionally fast, so eating on that day was one "violation" of tradition. Ham is a pork product, which is forbidden to Jews, so that's a second "violation." And having milk and meat together is also prohibited by Jewish dietary laws, making his offense a third "violation." His heretical trifecta is simply one example of how he observed his Judaism differently from my other friend.

3. A note about my terminology. When I talk about "many Jews" or "most Jews" I am specifically talking about non-Orthodox Jews. While up to three out of ten Israeli Jews would consider themselves some version of Orthodox or traditional (see Israel's population statistics from 2020,

see it as archaic or anachronistic. They do not believe the laws, rituals, and traditions speak to them in the twenty-first century. Ultimately, if someone doesn't find the relevance in something, no matter what it is, they will walk away from it. When you leave the snowy mountains, you shed your winter coat; and for many Jews today, Jewish tradition is a winter coat. A lack of basic Jewish literacy for so many Jews today is at the heart of this feeling of Judaism being irrelevant or archaic.

Second, we struggle to define "what" Judaism is today. Jewish identity is not as all-encompassing as it used to be. Before the Enlightenment in the mid-eighteenth century, if you were Jewish, it defined everything about you. It defined where you lived, how you dressed, what you ate, who you married, how you lived week to week and month to month, etc. Today, being Jewish could be just one small piece of your identity. Whereas in the past you were Jewish whether you chose to be or not, today it has been said that we are all Jews by choice. In Silicon Valley speak, Judaism used to be an "operating system," but for many today, it may just be one "app." So the "what" has become unanswerable for many Jews.

Finally, "how" we do Jewish today isn't working for many Jews. In the Diaspora, and especially here in America, for example, many Jews see Judaism as too tribalistic and overly ethnocentric. In an era when "universalism" is the driving ethos, ethnocentrism, particularism, and tribalism are looked

---

https://www.jewishvirtuallibrary.org/latest-population-statistics-for-israel), only nine percent of American Jews would call themselves Orthodox (see the Pew Research Center's 2020 survey, "Jewish Americans in 2020," https://www.pewforum.org/2021/05/11/jewish-americans-in-2020/.

down upon. And if someone falls in love, shouldn't all that matter be whether they're a good person and you share the same values? So, they ask, why must we do all that old-fashioned stuff, when we should all just be citizens of the world? In fact, Robert Mnookin based his book, *The Jewish American Paradox* on the conviction that the answers of the past no longer serve American Jews today.

In this book, I share my answers to these three core questions, and I pivot from asking "Why *be* Jewish?" to "Why *do* Jewish?". I do this by exploring how Judaism has evolved over three eras, from the time of Moses to the present, and share my belief that the Jewish People are on the eve of a fourth era. Though I am not entirely sure what that will look like, I share some ideas for how to help us evolve for the future.

The book is divided into three parts: Why Do Jewish; What Is Jewish; and How to Do Jewish. In chapter one, I offer my answer to the question at the heart of the book, which is, "Why do Jewish?" I share eight reasons for why I do Jewish, and then I share my thoughts on why Judaism offers an excellent answer to the meaning of life. Now if that isn't enough to motivate you to read on, then I don't know what is.

In chapter two, I begin exploring, "What is Jewish?" by describing the evolution of Jewish Peoplehood, and I divide this evolution into three eras:

1. Jewish Peoplehood 1.0 – the *Mishkan* period[4] when we were a wandering People

---

4. The *Mishkan* was the portable Holy Ark that traveled with the Jews as we wandered in the desert after the exodus from Egypt. Inside the Ark were the tablets that Moses received on Mt. Sinai.

2. Jewish Peoplehood 2.0 – the period of the Holy Temples when we were stationary
3. Jewish Peoplehood 3.0 – the current Diasporic period

Chapter three continues the exploration of "what" by proposing the notion that we are entering Judaism 4.0 – a new "operating system" for Jewish Peoplehood. I explore the five challenges facing Judaism today and why I believe we are at an inflection point. The five challenges are:
1. Dropping Institutional Affiliation
2. Shifting Jewish Ethnography
3. The Evolution of Israel-Diaspora Relations
4. A Broadened Search for Meaning And Belonging
5. Rapid Advances in Technology and Science

In chapter four, I pivot to the question of "How to do Jewish?" I start by proposing five responses to those five drivers of change. I make some bold predictions, so I expect this chapter may generate significant pushback, but that's okay, as I hope it creates conversation among those who care about the Jewish future. My five responses are:
1. David or Goliath? Betting on the Underdogs and Little Guys
2. Funny, You Don't Look Jewish: Embracing Radical Inclusivity
3. Z3: Evolving a Zionist Ideology for the Twenty-first Century
4. Making Our Own Shabbos: Reinventing Jewish Rituals and Holidays
5. Plugging In and Powering Up: Taking Advantage of Technology's Gifts

Chapter five continues the "how" by laying out a new framework for Jewish living based on the acronym TACHLIS, a Yiddish word meaning "getting down to business," or "talking brass tacks," that has been a driving force in my life – especially in moments when I feel like there is too much talking and not enough doing! In this context, TACHLIS stands for the following elements:

1. Tikkun Olam (Repairing the World)
2. Art and Culture
3. Community
4. Holidays and Rituals
5. Learning
6. Israel
7. Shabbat and Spirituality

Finally, in chapter six, I conclude the exploration of "How to do Jewish?" by sharing my thoughts on the Next Big Jewish Idea: a Jewish gap year between high school and college – or high school and the army in Israel – that becomes as normative as the bar or bat mitzvah has become for thirteen-year-old Jewish kids. I call it "The Jewish LEAP Year," and again, it is an acronym, which stands for: Learning, Experience, Action, and Peoplehood.

I end the book with an epilogue in which I tie it all together by proposing that Jewish Peoplehood could provide a path that would allow one to live a meaningful life. Indeed, it has done exactly that for me.

Throughout this book, I draw conclusions from nearly three decades of working, living, and volunteering in the Jewish community. I've been immersed in Orthodox settings and the secular world. I've spent time in academia, politics, and the non-profit world. I've lived in Israel and I've worked closely with Jews from around the world. In this book, I draw upon my own personal experiences from each of these different moments in my life.

I reference speakers, thinkers, books, lectures, and ancient Jewish texts where I can, but my commentary may not always reflect comprehensive data. This is not meant to be an academic work or philosophical tome. You will find my opinions intermingled with thoughts of much more renowned scholars, and naturally you will have differing opinions. You may even take offense at some comments, though I hope not. This book is meant to be a collection of my thoughts, impressions, reactions, experiences, and predictions.

Many of the ideas in this book have come out of my years running the Oshman Family JCC in Palo Alto, California. The OFJCC has been a wonderful incubator for new expressions of Jewish identity. (In fact, being such an incubator is one of our strategic pillars.) The JCC has been a place where the community can experiment with different types of Judaism, thanks in large part to the leadership which has been so open-minded about letting us try new things. My JCC colleagues have been my irreplaceable partners when it comes to thinking up new models for Jewish life, and they have been the ones to take the thoughts and turn them into action. From Z3 to LEAP Year to the entire TACHLIS framework, my colleagues have turned these ideas from dreams to reality, and the marketing team has been an ideal partner for helping wordsmith some of these creative acronyms.

I suppose what I'm trying to say is that many of the ideas in this book have benefitted from the creativity and ingenuity of thought partners and colleagues at the OFJCC, and I owe them all a tremendous debt of gratitude, since many of these ideas were formulated and nurtured by those on my OFJCC team.

Ultimately, this book is a manifesto – my manifesto – on how to make Jewish Peoplehood vital throughout this next century. It's my attempt to explain to my children, and hopefully to my grandchildren, why our Jewish heritage is important enough for us to shepherd it into the future. These are my own answers to the big questions, and if they resonate with others, then that's wonderful.

The ideas in this book likely may not sit well with the Orthodox community. But frankly, I don't believe the traditional Orthodox community is my audience, since they do not seem to need convincing as to why and how to find meaning and relevance in Jewish life – they already have. And for those in that community who are indeed searching, they might find answers here. So, while I hope I don't offend my Orthodox brothers and sisters, I hope they will understand the reason I'm writing this book and the audience I am targeting.

I need to offer one last caveat. I am pluralist at heart, which means I believe there are many paths to truth. I don't believe there is only one right path, and in fact, I don't believe there is only one truth. There are many paths and multiple truths. The ideas in this book happen to make up the path that works for me and may work for others, but it is just one of many.

To that end, I'd like to hear your thoughts. Please share your own paths and truths with me. Share your own ideas for why doing Jewish matters to you. Share your impressions of my take on this moment in Jewish history, and whether you have a different one. If you have a story that transformed your life Jewishly, I'd love to hear it. Please engage with me on this subject, as it's the back-and-forth that brings these ideas to life. Like a modern Talmud, let's interpret and reinterpret each other's insights together.

If you're interested, you can reach me at:
www.zackbodner.com or www.whydojewish.com.

PART 1
WHY DO JEWISH?

1

The Meaning of Life

In the spring of 2020, the world went into lockdown because of the global COVID19 pandemic. It just so happened that this was when my son, Elie, was supposed to celebrate his bar mitzvah. We struggled with whether to postpone the celebration or continue virtually. In the end, we decided to host a Zoom bar mitzvah and are so glad we did. It was a wonderful experience – not only for my son and my family, but for the more than three hundred people who attended online.[1]

The Torah portion for my son's bar mitzvah was *Behar-Bechukotai*. It's a double portion in which we learn about God commanding us to let the earth rest for a Yovel (jubilee) year. Just like people, the earth needs time to rest and reset. Humans need it every seven days, but the earth needs it every seven years; and every seven times seven years – forty-nine years – we need to really let the earth rest, so that becomes

---

1. If you are interested, you can read about it in an article I wrote for *The Forward*: "How a Silcon Valley Mindset Helped Us Host an Epic Zoom Bar Mitzvah," June 24, 2020, https://forward.com/scribe/449455/how-a-silicon-valley-mindset-helped-us-host-an-epic-zoom-bar-mitzvah/. If you'd actually like to watch the ceremony, you can find it at https://www.youtube.com/watch?v=OlN8gikVn-Q.

a two-year rest period, with the fiftieth year celebrated as a Yovel year.

In the Torah portion, we learn about all the ways we are supposed to let the earth rest, then we learn how we will be blessed if we do, and finally we read about all the curses that will befall us if we don't – and that list of curses is terrifying. For instance, God says the following:

> But if you do not obey Me and will not do all these com-mandments...I also will do this to you: I will appoint terror over you – even consumption and fever, that shall make the eyes to fail and the soul to languish.... I will make your heaven like iron and your earth like brass.... your land shall not yield its produce, nor shall the trees of the land yield their fruit ... I will send the beast of the field among you, which shall rob you of your children, and destroy your cattle, and make you few in number; and your roads shall become deso-late.... and you will be gathered together within your cities; and I will send the pestilence among you; and you will be delivered into the hand of the enemy.... And if you will not for all this obey Me, but walk contrary unto Me, then I will walk contrary unto you in fury....[2]

Ominous, right? As I was reading this, I realized that we may actually be experiencing Divine wrath in the form of COVID19 because we've ignored the commandment to let the earth rest. In fact, we have made the earth suffer with no reprieve. We are polluting our skies as well as our water supplies. We

---

2. Leviticus 26:14–28.

are burning down our forests and eroding our beaches. We are killing off wild animals and torturing domesticated ones in the name of "food." We are over-populating cities and destroying the ozone. And now we are experiencing the curses that follow our actions.

When I shared these thoughts with my wife in the initial draft of my speech for my son's bar mitzvah, she sardonically suggested that the tone might be a little too dark for the joyous occasion. Thankfully, I listened to her advice and offered a much more uplifting message. But it didn't stop me from wondering whether this global pandemic is indeed forcing us to reap what we've sown.

As it has for so many moments in time, Jewish tradition has something to say about this particular time. Jewish wisdom calls us to be true to certain values. Jewish sages have insights and advice. Jewish stories share morals and teachings. If we look for it in our shared Jewish memory, we can find meaning in this very moment, too.

Start with the WHY

The author and inspirational speaker Simon Sinek has motivated millions of people to think about the purpose, cause, or belief that drives every one of us. He calls it "the WHY," and gave a famous TED talk called "Start with the Why" in which he describes the Golden Circle.[3] In it, he talks about how great leaders inspire action by motivating people based on *why*

---

3.   Simon Sinek, "How Great Leaders Inspire Action," filmed September 2009 at TEDxPugetSound, Newcastle, WA, video, 17:49, https://www.ted.com/talks/simon_sinek_how_great_leaders_inspire_action .

they should do something. The Golden Circle has three rings: the outermost concentric circle contains the "what," while the next layer in contains the "how," and the innermost circle contains the "why." Great leaders talk about *why* we must do what we do because that's what inspires action, that's what is memorable, and that's what gives meaning to the doing.

When I searched for all the books on Amazon.com entitled "Why Be Jewish?," my query revealed four books and a short pamphlet:

- *Why Be Jewish? A Testament* by Edgar M. Bronfman, published in 2016.
- *Why Be Jewish? Knowledge and Inspiration for Jews of Today* by Doron Kornbluth, published in 2011.
- *Why Be Jewish?* by David J. Wolpe, published in 1995.
- *Why Be Jewish? Intermarriage, Assimilation, and Alienation* by Meir Kahane, published in 1977.
- *Why Be Jewish? (Jewish Identity Today)*, a short pamphlet by Barry W. Holtz, published by the American Jewish Committee in 1993.

Each book has something different to say about the topic, and each says it in a different way. One is a spiritual love poem to his faith, while another is a call to arms for Jews to fight for their Jewishness. One puts the reader in a different person's shoes in each chapter, and another is a man's final testimony before he died.

The magnate-philanthropist Edgar Bronfman's book, published only weeks before he passed away, is a collection of lessons from his life that have been woven together "to encourage others to take another look at their tradition and craft a practice of their own, one that need not include belief in a traditional God."[4]

Doron Kornbluth, a speaker, author, and Israeli tour guide, wrote a book in which he seeks to "reflect the multiplicity of our Jewish experiences and outlooks"[5] by taking on different voices in each of the nineteen chapters, each of which is a separate essay that, when put together, attempt to answer the question, "How does my Jewish identity fit in with my other definitions (American. British. Israeli. Male. Female. Vegetarian. Mets fan. Democrat. Republican...)?"[6]

Meanwhile, Rabbi David Wolpe, the senior rabbi at Sinai Temple in Los Angeles, wrote what is essentially a love poem to Judaism and suggests that his short, inspiring book is "a personal portrait of faith for those who are searching: an attempt to show in quick, large strokes what this remarkable faith is really about and how it can transform your life."[7]

Finally, Meir Kahane, whose thought-leadership has been rejected by mainstream Judaism in the last more than thirty years due to his racist ideologies, wrote a harsh critique of intermarriage, assimilation, and life in the Diaspora, calling his book: "A battle plan for Jews who do not want to disappear."[8]

In this manifesto, however, I am pivoting from the question "Why *be* Jewish?" to "Why *do* Jewish?" It may sound like

---

4. Edgar M. Bronfman, *Why Be Jewish?: A Testament* (New York: Twelve, 2016), 6.
5. Doron Kornbluth, *Why Be Jewish: Knowledge and Inspiration for Jews of Today* (Beit Shemesh, Israel: Mosaica Press, 2011), 9.
6. Kornbluth, *Why Be Jewish*, 22.
7. David Wolpe, *Why Be Jewish?* (New York: Owl Books, 1995), xiv.
8. Meir Kahane, *Why Be Jewish: Intermarriage, Assimilation, and Alienation* (BN Publishing, 1977), from the endorsement page.

improper grammar (please don't tell my mother, the retired English teacher), but I believe the word "Jewish" should be a noun as much as it's been an adjective. Although Merriam-Webster Dictionary might not agree with me, thought leaders like Rabbi Noa Kushner of The Kitchen in San Francisco have been using the term "doing Jewish" for years now. Today, in the twenty-first century, living Jewishly ought to mean more than who your mother was. Doing Jewish means taking some specific actions, living by some specific values, celebrating some specific moments, and recognizing you are part of some specific family.

I say "some" because I don't believe you must take *all* the actions prescribed by the rabbis to live a Jewish life. But I also don't believe you can ignore all of them and still consider yourself to be living a Jewish life. Rabbi David Wolpe spoke at the OFJCC and asked the group, "If someone were investigating you and trying to prove you were Jewish, how long would it take them to find evidence? What Jewish items are in your home – books, pictures, mail, Judaica on the shelves? What do you wear that makes it clear you're Jewish? What do you do on a regular basis that is clearly Jewish?"

For me, there are some Jewish actions I must take, and determining which actions those are has been a lifelong journey of discovery for me. Admittedly, I'm still on that journey, so those actions continue to change, but as long as I'm checking off some of the items on that "to-do" list, I can affirm that I'm *doing* Jewish.

Choosing to *do* Jewish is a conscious choice, while I can't choose to *be* Jewish, just as I can't choose to be member of my family. I just am. I was born that way. There's nothing I can do to change that. I can extract myself from my family by actively doing things to walk away from them, but I'll always be the child of my parents, the grandchild of my grandparents, and of course, the parent to my own children. I can alienate myself with my actions, but my DNA will always make me a part of my family, whether I like it or not. And believe me, after some of our Passover Seders debating politics with my family members, I'm not always sure how we share any DNA at all, but it's still my family no matter what.

Of course, one can convert into Judaism. Someone can choose to be Jewish in the positive by going through a conversion process. But the rabbis say you can't ever convert out of Judaism. You can try, but you'll still always be Jewish. In fact, Rabbi Eliezer Yehuda Waldenberg shares a story in which a Jewish woman converted to Christianity in order to marry a Christian man, but wanted to convert back to Judaism after expressing remorse. Rabbi Waldenberg ruled that, "Against his will, a Jew remains a Jew, connected to the religion of Moses, with no recourse to free himself from it." He goes on to say that this woman never left Judaism, therefore, she had no need to convert back because "her return to Judaism is like the return of a daughter to her mother."[9]

So, for me, it's more interesting to answer the question, "Why do Jewish?"

Why I Do Jewish

First, I do Jewish because it provides a compelling worldview. I see the world and my place in it through a Jewish lens. How I engage with the world around me, including other people, is

---

9.   Tzitz Eliezer 13:93.

based on my Jewish overview. To be more specific, the guiding principle that drives my behavior is based on the very simple *platinum* rule, as put forth by Rabbi Hillel: Don't do to others what you wouldn't want them to do to you. It's not the golden rule, which is stated in the positive – do for others what you would want them to do for you; it's the corollary, stated in the reverse, which obliges us to actively put ourselves in the shoes of others.

There is a famous story in the Talmud about a potential convert to Judaism approaching Rabbi Hillel and saying, "I'll convert to Judaism if you can share the entire Torah standing on one foot." Hillel replies without missing a beat, "What is hateful to you, do not do unto others. That is the whole Torah, the rest is commentary. Now go learn them."[10]

Judaism is about doing what's right – what's right for you, for others, and for the world. If it's not right for you, then surely it can't be right for others. So, don't do it. It's just that simple. And Judaism manifests that ethos beautifully. Of course, many have perverted that today, but I still hold to the central tenet that Hillel shared with that curious potential convert that day: If your momma wouldn't want you to do it, then don't do it!

Second, I do Jewish because its values are timeless guardrails for how to live a good life. Values like repair the world, be a light unto the nations, beat swords into plowshares, take care of the stranger, lift up the fallen, show gratitude, embrace diversity, protect the environment, step away from work every week, remember the past, all people are made in the Divine image, teach your children, be there for your community,

---

10. Talmud, *Shabbat* 31a.

ask questions, be a *mensch* (a good person), along with so many others, are values that guide me on my journey. They tie together to create my worldview the way trees make up a forest and provide a path that allows me to live a life filled with purpose.

You could tell me that all religions offer guardrails, and I'd agree with you. And you could say some religion's guardrails might even be better than Judaism's guardrails. And though you might be right, I haven't found values in other religions that improve on Judaism's. I've studied a fair number of other religions, and I like many of them. I have found many of them offer a compelling worldview with values that might allow one to live a meaningful and fulfilling life. But Judaism is the right one for me; it's mine.

In his book *A Letter in the Scroll*, Rabbi Jonathan Sacks explains it in a way that fully resonates with me. He asks us to imagine that we are in a vast library with books from floor to ceiling, with information about all sorts of lifestyles. He says we may choose from any of the books and thus, any of the various life paths. We can try them, and then we are free to change them when they no longer suit us. Then he says the following:

> Judaism asks us to envisage an altogether different possibility. Imagine that, while browsing in the library, you come across one book unlike the rest, which catches your eye because on its spine is written the name of your family. Intrigued, you open it and see many pages written by different hands in many languages. You start reading it, and gradually you begin to understand what it is. It is the story each generation

of your ancestors has told for the sake of the next, so that everyone born into this family can learn where they came from, what happened to them, what they lived for and why. As you turn the pages, you reach the last, which carries no entry but a heading. It bears your name....

Seeing my name and the story of my forebears, I could not read it as if it were just one story among others; instead, reading it would inevitably become, for me, a form of self-discovery. Once I knew that it existed, I could not put the book back on the shelf and forget it, because I would know that I am part of a long line of people who traveled toward a certain destination and whose journey remains unfinished, dependent on me to take it further.[11]

Third, I do Jewish because our heritage is rich and filled with wonderful wisdom that makes me proud and speaks to me. Our ancient texts are filled with incredible stories, customs, and laws that the rabbis in each generation make relevant for modern times. The commentaries written by the sages in each successive generation have only added to the richness of those texts. Then the fables and folktales similarly have so much to teach us, while also entertaining us. Even the modern Jewish canon has so much to say about how to live a good life. Our tradition tells us to build on those who have come before us and prepare for the future.

There is a famous talmudic story of Honi the Circle Maker

---

11. Rabbi Jonathan Sacks, *A Letter in the Scroll* (New York: The Free Press, 2000), 43–44.

who sees a man planting a carob tree and asks the man how long it takes to bear fruit. The man replies that it takes seventy years, to which Honi replies, "Are you certain that you will live another seventy years?" And the man says, "I found carob trees in this world planted for me by my ancestors, so I am planting these for my descendants."[12]

This is a wonderful example of how a nugget of wisdom is shared in the Jewish tradition. Honi the Circle Maker shows up as the protagonist in several stories in the Talmud, always entertaining us and simultaneously teaching us an important lesson. This is not unique to Judaism, of course. Every people has their stories, folklore, fables, legends, and oral traditions – and many of them are truly wonderful. However, Jewish wisdom speaks to me in a unique way, as it has been passed down to me from my parents and their parents and their parents before them.

Fourth, I do Jewish because the rituals, customs, and holidays provide a framework to how I live my weeks, months, and years. The Jewish calendar honors the cycles of nature while also acknowledging human nature. Our need to unplug, recharge, and rest every week is why I honor and remember Shabbat. Our need to self-reflect and set new goals for ourselves is part of the *cheshbon hanefesh* I do during Rosh Hashanah and Yom Kippur annually.[13] Meanwhile, telling the story of the Exodus from Egypt during the Passover Seder in the first person allows me every year to think about what I must liberate myself from in that very moment and connects

---

12. Talmud, *Taanit* 23a.
13. *Cheshbon hanefesh* means an accounting of the soul.

me to my ancestors in a tangible way. Even the way Judaism has a ritual to mark important lifecycle moments is profound – from birth to adolescence to marriage to death.

For example, during the global Coronavirus pandemic, my wife and I were forced to work from home. It didn't take long before we were asking ourselves if we were working from home or living at work. Our days started to blend together as there was no difference between Monday, Thursday, or Saturday. We often found ourselves sitting on our computers and doing work on our weekends, which is something we rarely did when we worked at our offices. After a while, it felt like we were always working and never taking a break. I know this is the very reason why Shabbat is so essential. It is a way to differentiate our days and give ourselves a break. While I haven't perfected this yet, I'm working on it. But the idea of Shabbat as a weekly cleansing, a weekly refresh, and a differentiator is profound and speaks deeply to me.

Fifth, I do Jewish because it evokes strong memories for me. I hear my own family's history in the stories shared by Jewish storytellers. I feel nostalgic when I eat bagels and lox on a Sunday morning, and I feel inspired when I eat falafel and hummus at the local falafel stand in Tel Aviv. I love singing Shabbat songs on Friday night around the dinner table, where I bless my kids the way my father blessed me. Even collective memories of experiences I haven't personally had inspire nostalgia for me. When I hear how the young, pioneering kibbutzniks settled the land of Israel in the early twentieth century amidst so much hardship, I feel like I was there alongside them. That is part of my story too, and I can feel it.

Take the following story, for example. My father-in-law was born in Palestine in 1938 to a Sephardic Jewish family that fled Thessalonika, Greece, to escape the Nazis. His family supported the more hawkish underground Jewish liberators, the Irgun, who not only fought the British occupiers but also the more liberal underground Jewish fighters, the Haganah. My father-in-law was not yet ten years old when Israel fought its battle for independence, and he remembers standing on the beaches of Tel Aviv watching as Haganah fighters fired on an Irgun weapons ship, sinking the ship along with valuable weapons and killing some of the men onboard. That memory is not only seared into my father-in-law's brain, but it's now part of my collective memory as well. I can see it as clearly as if I were standing on that beach, too.

Sixth, I do Jewish because so much of the culture fills me with joy. It is fun. I love the subtle Jewish symbolism, I understand the inside jokes, and I relate to the neurosis of Jewish comedians. I enjoy the wordplays by Jewish authors. I appreciate the symbolism in Jewish art. I savor the Jewish food, even if my arteries don't. I love the holidays and the rituals. I love dancing the hora and lifting people on chairs at every celebratory rite of passage.

For instance, how can you not love Purim? Purim is a holiday that celebrates the Jews evading genocide by the Persian king's right-hand man, Haman, in the fourth century BCE thanks to the queen, Ester, and her uncle, Mordechai. And how are we commanded to celebrate this holiday? Yes, of course we retell the story – that's an integral component to all our holidays – and yes, we feast on a big meal – that too is an important part of many of our holidays. But we are also commanded to get so drunk we can't tell the difference between good and evil, between Mordechai and Haman. What other religion commands you to get drunk like that? Like I said, doing Jewish can be fun.

Seventh, I do Jewish because it makes me feel connected to a larger family. When Jews in other parts of the world experience troubles, I empathize deeply with them. Similarly, when Jews excel and receive accolades, I feel a sense of pride as if they were a member of my family. How many times have I listened to Adam Sandler's Hanukkah songs and smiled? How many times have I stood up a little taller when another Jew wins the Nobel Prize? When I meet strangers and we get to know each other, if I learn that they are Jewish I immediately feel a deeper connection. And when I travel, I visit the local synagogue or JCC to understand what's happening there to *my* people.

As the CEO of the OFJCC in Palo Alto, I am lucky enough to be a member of JCC Global, a network of JCCs around the world. This provides wonderful insight into what's happening to other Jewish communities, but it also connects me to new colleagues and friends all over the globe. Now, whenever I'm traveling to a foreign country, I will reach out beforehand to make a connection, like I did several years ago before traveling to Spain.

In the spring of 2018, my family and I traveled with another family to Barcelona for Passover break. We needed a place to have a Seder, so I reached out to my friends at JCC Global for a connection to the Barcelona Jewish community. Sure enough, they connected me, and I made plans for us to join a Passover Seder at the local JCC. When we arrived, we had to go through a security screening (such is the sad state for Jews these days) and then we joined the community downstairs for their annual celebration. Our group of ten filled an entire table, but our hosts placed us near another table of Americans. As we started schmoozing, I engaged in one of my favorite party games, Jewish Geography, and it didn't take five minutes before one of the other guests said she heard me speak at a synagogue, while another guest discovered she knew my friend's mother, as they both immigrated to the US from Russia around the same time. That's what it means to feel connected to a larger family.

Finally, I do Jewish because it gives my life meaning. I believe Judaism has something unique to say about the meaning of life. There are three big questions we must answer in life. The first, is "Who am I?" The second is, "Why am I here?" And the third is, "What is my task?"[14] Judaism answers those questions for me. And at the end of the day, living a meaningful, purpose-driven life is what it's all about, isn't it?

So then, what is the meaning of life? Well, I'm glad you asked…

The Meaning of Life

I have always been a searcher. My story isn't an exodus story or a redemption story, but a wilderness story. I studied psychology of religion in college, hoping to discover the intrinsic motivation of religiousness. I wanted to know why humans have always sought a Higher Power, a Greater Source, an Answer to the all-consuming question of why we exist.

---

14. These questions have been posed by a variety of philosophers in a number of variations, but I've chosen the formulation offered by Rabbi Jonathan Sacks in his book *Lessons in Leadership: A Weekly Reading of the Jewish Bible* (Jerusalem: Maggid Books, 2015), 276. However, I've chosen to list them in the singular "I" rather than the plural "we" for sake of emphasis.

When I didn't find my answer in a liberal arts university, I spent some time studying at a yeshiva in Jerusalem. There at Ohr Somayach, they had answers. They had answers to all the questions, including the ones I hadn't even thought to ask. But the dogmatic nature of their answers didn't always feel right to me.

Then I went to graduate school to study philosophy of religion and theology. I thought maybe a more secular, yet focused pursuit to the answer to the meaning of life could be found there. But here too I was unsatisfied. The answers were less dogmatic, but they still didn't fully resonate with me. Ultimately, I felt I could not discover an answer to the meaning of life in an academic setting.

I was impatient. I wanted answers, but I wanted to make change, too. I wanted to see results. So, I made the shift to politics, hoping that I could be the change I wanted to see in the world and that through the *doing*, perhaps I could discover the meaning – like the biblical advice, "*naaseh v'nishma*";[15] if we *do* it first – sometimes without even knowing why – then after, sometimes we can *hear*, or understand, why we are meant to do it.

I earned a fellowship and began working in Sacramento for a state senator. He was a great visionary who strove to bring peace – peace between inner-city gangs in LA, peace between Catholics and Protestants in Northern Ireland, and peace between the rich and poor in America. I saw poverty, suffering, and the intractability of conflict. I saw how slow it can be to create real resolution. I learned the difference between what

---

15. Exodus 24:7.

Yehuda Kurtzer has called "Messianic Politics" and "Exodus Politics." Messianic political change is revolutionary, cyclical, and violent, and it feels good but doesn't always last; while Exodus political change takes time and is slower but ultimately brings you through the wilderness to the promised land.

Then late one night, I was lying in bed – which was really just a mattress sitting flat on the floor – staring up at the ceiling, unable to sleep, thinking about why all these people had to suffer, why the world was created if people were just going to experience pain, wondering what was life really all about anyway. A funk had been building in my soul over the last few months as I'd been seeing so much hardship in the world. I feared I was falling into a depression and I wanted to scream out, "What the hell is it all for?!"

Then all of a sudden it hit me. Really! Out of nowhere, the answer came to me. It was like the cliché of a bolt of lightning, and I realized suddenly why the world exists and what the meaning of life is.

Now stick with me, because I know this might sound a little hokey. Even though I don't believe God is an old man in white robes actually up in the sky pulling the strings, this is really how it came to me, so what am I supposed to do? I have to tell it like it happened, so here goes...

I suddenly had this epiphany that eons ago, the Great Divine Force was up there all alone in the cosmos enjoying the perfect life, nirvana, paradise, and decided to share this perfect experience. God no longer wanted to keep it all in this Divine Space, and that's when God decided to make the world and create human beings. The Divine Source of all life wanted to share nirvana with another soul that could appreciate it.[16]

I felt as if God's decision was analogous to how I love to travel to new places and experience the world. It's one thing to have those adventures on my own, but it can reach another level altogether when I share them with someone else. When I have a partner, I have someone with whom I can share the experience, someone with whom I can reminisce afterward, someone with whom I can laugh and say, "Hey, remember that time when..." When I travel on my own I don't have that opportunity, so it's just a little less than perfect. That's how I thought God must have felt at that moment when the decision was made to create the universe.

In Jewish tradition, it wasn't that *nothing* existed before God created the world. It was that God existed, and *only* God existed. So, to make space for anything and everything else, the Divine Force had to contract part of God's Self to make space for the rest. I think of it like sucking in my stomach to make space on a crowded elevator.

The Jewish mystics call this first step in the act of creation *tzimtzum*, which means to shrink, and it's the most selfless act that could ever occur: this act of contracting part of one's self to make space for something else. And that's what God did. After contracting, God created the universe in that empty space.[17]

---

16. Just to be clear, I believe in science and evolution. So, when I say that God created the world and human beings, I don't mean to suggest God created them at the same time in their current form. Of course, both the earth and human life evolved over time, but God's sense of time and our sense of time are not the same.

17. Likutei Moharan 64:1.

That act of creation, that moment when the universe came into being, was simultaneously an act of destruction. Why? Because no object is strong enough to hold the Essence of God, the Intentionality of The One, the full Force of the Universe. So, the "vessels" that God created to hold this Divine light shattered, and those shards exploded throughout the universe. And it is our job to find those shards and put them back together.

Our role in existence is to recapture the Divine light and bring it back into the world. We exist as partners in creation with God. We exist to bring back the light.

The term *tikkun olam* means "repairing the world," and while it can be originally sourced in the Mishnah, it is also tied to the story of *tzimtzum*. It means finding those shards and piecing them back together. So Tikkun Olam is truly what we are meant to do in the world – to repair the world, to make it a better place.

When it comes to our purpose and the meaning of life, nobody said it better than Abraham Joshua Heschel: "God is in search of man."[18] God needs us. Human beings must exist so God's work can be done. If people doesn't exist, then only God exists, all alone. So, we exist to do God's work, to be God's partners in creation, to finish the work of the Divine, and to bring God's holiness into the everyday world.

The Source of all life created the world to share with us humans the nirvana that God was experiencing. Our job is to experience that nirvana and help create it for others. Our purpose in living is to experience joy and to bring joy to others.

---

18. Abraham Joshua Heschel, *God in Search of Man* (New York: Farrar, Straus, and Giroux, 1976), 136.

This is the meaning of life: to create joy in the world.

We do this by making the world a better place. By fixing the problems we see. By righting the wrongs. By bringing justice. By alleviating suffering. By being *mensches* in the world. Rabbi Arthur Green writes in *Radical Judaism*, "We have emerged as partners of the One in the survival and maintenance of this planet and all the precious attainments that have evolved here."[19] So, if we can improve the world for living creatures, then those creatures will have a greater sense of joy. Thus, our actions will have caused more joy in the world.

All of us were put here on this earth to be God's partners in creation, to be God's partners in repairing the world, but the Jews were put here with a specific role in this partnership. We are meant to be the catalyst for making change. We are meant to be the ones leading the charge as we all work to put together the broken pieces of the vessels that hold the Divine light. The Jews are the tip of the spear in this fight. We are meant to be a light unto the nations by bringing light *to* the nations. That's why the Jews are often so engaged with causes that improve society. (And unfortunately, it's also why the Jews are so often the targets of hatred and bigotry – people don't like to have flaws pointed out to them. But this isn't a discussion of antisemitism. Others, like the scholar Deborah Lipstadt and journalist Bari Weiss, have done an excellent job of tackling that subject.)

The author Douglas Rushkoff, in his book *Nothing Sacred: The Truth About Judaism*, says the reason why Jews so often

---

19. Arthur Green, *Radical Judaism: Rethinking God and Tradition* (New Haven: Yale University Press, 2010), 27.

are optimists and activists is because of this need to be God's partners in creation. He writes:

> We have assumed a responsibility that many others have deferred to God. Some of us re-create God's creative work through ritual, while others adopt a more participatory model of ongoing creation through the performance of good works. In either case, the Jewish difference is to engage consciously in the writing of ourstory.[20]

Now you might challenge by asking, "But why must there be any problems at all, any wrongs, any injustice? Shouldn't God have created a perfect world?"

First, I am not sure all of that was in God's control. Yes, I know that sounds counterintuitive. But again, I don't believe in the notion of God as an all-knowing, all-controlling being up there pulling the strings. I believe a Great Force, the Oneness of All Things, launched creation, and then certain reactions occurred. Planets were birthed. Life evolved. And some of those reactions weren't necessarily positive from a human perspective. In fact, some Jewish mystics believe the universe was created over nine hundred times before God settled on this version, as imperfect as it is. But of course, we can't begin to know what the Big Plan really is, since we are only human.

Second, we have to be active partners in creation. We wouldn't have anything to do if the world was fully created and it was perfect. We wouldn't have any role other than to

---

20. Douglas Rushkoff, *Nothing Sacred: The Truth About Judaism* (New York: Crown Publishers, 2003), 194.

just sit back and enjoy. And just as we teach our children they must work hard to truly appreciate the fruits of their labor or they will take for granted the things that are given to them, we too need to work hard to perfect our world. We would not appreciate it if it were simply given to us. Rabbi Daniel Gordis writes in *God Was Not in the Fire*, "We are, our tradition suggests, a people constantly searching for the Promised Land, knowing that the most enriching part of our lives may be this process of searching, not necessarily the exhilaration of arriving."[21] In fact, I think that's what the Garden of Eden story is really saying: when we were given perfection, we didn't appreciate it and we took it for granted. So, we lost it.

Third, one must experience sadness to know happiness. And yes, unfortunately, there must be wrong so we can know what's right. This is not meant to rationalize all the suffering, pain, and evil in the world. I am not attempting to answer that age-old question – which others have done better than I can – namely, "Why do bad things happen to good people?"[22] But I do believe we need darkness to see light, as in the second section of the *Toa Te Ching*, which declares:

> Recognize beauty and ugliness is born; Recognize good and evil is born. Is and Isn't produce each other. Hard depends on easy. Long is tested by short. High is determined by low.[23]

---

21. Daniel Gordis, *God Was Not in the Fire: The Search for a Spiritual Judaism* (New York: Scribner, 1995), 45.
22. For an answer to this question, try *When Bad Things Happen to Good People* by Harold S. Kushner (New York: Anchor Books, 2004).
23. Lao-tzu, *Tao Te Ching*, trans. Stephen Addiss and Stanley Lombardo (Indianapolis: Hackett Publishing Company, 1993), 2.

That may not be a satisfying answer, so let me offer another one from a wise sage whom I've already quoted, Rabbi Jonathan Sacks. During the pandemic, Rabbi Sacks said the following:

> God does not want us to understand why bad things happen to good people. Because if we understood, we would be forced to accept that bad things happen to good people. And God does not want us to accept those bad things. He wants us not to understand so that we will fight against the bad and the injustices of this world. And that is why there is no answer to that question. Because God has arranged that we shall never have an answer to that question.[24]

Finally, I want to acknowledge that in truth, I *know* nothing about this. I only have my own *beliefs* and *ideas*. For how can we, as humans, be fully capable of grasping Divine purpose? Of course, we can't; and I would be highly skeptical of anyone who says otherwise.

But I do believe what the ancient Jewish mystics recognized – that by contracting a part of our own selves, by giving something of ourselves the way God did in the creation of the world, we are being Godlike. And that is the ultimate goal of life – to be like God.

We are meant to experience joy and create joy in the world, even by giving something of ourselves. Some talk of living a life of "service," which is the notion of giving something

---

24. Rabbi Jonathan Sacks, interview by Rivkah Krinsky and Eda Schottenstein, *From the Inside Out*, podcast audio, September 11, 2020.

of one's self for the benefit of another. And some use the word "love" in place of joy, but they are similar ideas in my mind. Spread the love. Spread the light. Spread the joy – and not in a hedonistic way, but by doing the work that makes the world a better place.

The Jewish educator Avraham Infeld sums it up beautifully in his book *A Passion for a People* when he says:

> Is there any point in being Jewish without aiming to improve the world? None of the other things we do as Jews have ultimate purpose; the only thing that gives us that ultimate purpose is looking outward to make a difference in the world. God created an incomplete world, and it is our job to complete it.[25]

This is the underlying belief, the core conviction, indeed the entirety of this manifesto standing on one foot. This is the engine that can drive the deeper purpose of Jewish Peoplehood for the twenty-first century. This is what can inspire our children and our children's children to keep doing Jewish: the recognition that we exist for the holy purpose of repairing the world.

So, there you have it, the meaning of life as informed by Jewish mysticism and theology. I have found much peace of mind in this notion. Of course, not every day has been pure bliss since I discovered this answer. I still fret and worry and grow melancholy way too often. I still struggle with impatience and defensiveness and anger. I still wrestle with God

---

25. Avraham Infeld, *A Passion for A People: Lessons from the Life of a Jewish Educator* (Jerusalem: Melitz, 2017), 138–39.

all the time. But you do know that the name Israel means "to wrestle with God," right? How appropriate is that?!

And of course, I still question. A lot. But now I also know those feelings will eventually pass, and I will once again actively seek joy. Because what else is there if not making meaning by creating joy in life?

PART 2
WHAT IS JEWISH?

2

Why Is This Night Different from All Other Nights?

I love bacon. Or at least, I used to love bacon back when I ate bacon...and pepperoni pizza and spare ribs and moo-shoo pork. But I stopped eating *treif* as a New Year's resolution in December of 1994 after I returned from studying abroad in Israel and wanted a way to hold on to my experience. Now, over twenty-five years later, married with three children, I still stick to it. We don't eat *treif*...at least, not in the house.

Okay, yes, I know there are a few inconsistencies in my philosophy. But like Ralph Waldo Emerson said, "A foolish consistency is the hobgoblin of little minds." (By the way, do you think hobgoblin are *treif*?)

As I mentioned, this is how I was raised: no pepperoni pizza in the house, but moo-shoo pork at the local Chinese restaurant on Sunday night was okay (as long as we didn't bring home any leftovers). And now we do it similarly in my family. No *treif* in the house. Though we have taken it one step further: we also don't eat anything that went "oink" outside the house as well. (Shellfish is okay, however, as we call this "Pacific Northwest Kosher.") But since my kids have been receiving a Jewish day school education, they are old enough and smart enough to ask the tough questions, challenge their parents, and put us on the hot seat with our inconsistencies – which is really why we pay so much money for them to go to Jewish day school, right?

A few years ago, we were with my extended family over Thanksgiving – including the three step-siblings who married non-Jews. We were having Sunday brunch at a restaurant, sitting outside enjoying the Arizona sunshine, sipping Bloody Marys made from the roll-right-up-to-your-table-Bloody Mary cart. My step-siblings all had giant strips of bacon standing next to the celery stalks in their drinks, and when they heard that my oldest daughter, Talia, who was twelve at the time, had never tasted bacon before, they began baiting her mercilessly. She looked at me, not knowing what to do. She knows the rules of *kashrut*; she knows we don't eat bacon in our family; but here were her aunts and uncles daring her to try it.

I could tell she was torn, so I said to her, "You are about to have your bat mitzvah. You are learning the different ways Jews do Jewish and what being Jewish means to you. And I think you are old enough to make your own decisions about how you want to do Jewish."

I explained to her why we don't eat bacon, and continued, "If you want to try bacon, you can. And then you should make up your own mind as to whether you want to keep eating bacon or not. But know this one thing: bacon is delicious."

A couple hundred years ago, it would have been unheard of for Jews to eat bacon. Eating any *treif* would have been the equivalent of leaving Judaism. Jews would have seen that person as no longer Jewish, and non-Jews would have likely agreed. But now it's so common for Jews to eat *treif* and still consider themselves fully, unabashedly, and unapologetically Jewish, that I would bet fewer Jews in the world actually keep kosher than don't – including me.

A couple hundred years ago, if you were Jewish it defined everything about you. Judaism was your singular Operating System. Just like you can't run Windows on an iPhone, Jews could not eat *treif* and still be Jewish. In fact, if you chose to do Jewish at all differently than what was prescribed, then you were choosing to leave Judaism. And if you had trouble making that choice known to the community, then the arbiters of Judaism would help make the choice for you. (If you want a refresher course on how it was several generations back, I encourage you to watch *Fiddler On The Roof* and you'll see how a community of Jews – including a distraught father – reacted to children doing something not in accordance to the Jewish way.)

Of course, some Jewish communities still operate this way. But the vast majority of non-traditional Jews are not quite so dogmatic. They recognize that Jews can do Jewish differently and still be Jewish. The arbiters of Jewish tradition may not like it. They may prefer that we do Jewish in a way that looks more like they do it. But they would reluctantly agree that a Jew who doesn't eat kosher or keep Shabbat or marry another Jewish person is still a Jew if they were born to a Jewish mother.

So then, that begs the question: is Judaism still an Operating System? Or has Judaism shifted to being an app? Or is it a folder of apps?

Before I dive into answering that question, I will finish my opening story. My daughter Talia did in fact try the bacon at our family brunch that Thanksgiving. Much to my surprise, she was underwhelmed and decided that turkey bacon was just as good as the real thing, so it wasn't worth breaking tradition. I suppose I'm grateful that the bacon she tried was a little soggy from tomato juice, making it much less tasty than I remember bacon being!

What Is Judaism?

Judaism is over three thousand years old, but is there any single, agreed-upon definition of what Judaism actually is? Here is a multiple-choice test for you. Is Judaism:
1. A religion?
2. A nationality?
3. A moral code?
4. A culture?

The answer is all of the above ... and none of the above.

For four hundred years, from 1492 through the late 1800s, Spain persecuted Jews even if they converted to Catholicism. It wasn't enough that Jews gave up their religious practices and pledged their faith to the Catholic Church. Judaism was seen as something more than religion, something deeper than religion.

You might argue, "Well, that ended over 150 years ago when the Inquisition ended." But even today, the latest studies show that only eleven percent of American Jews see their own Judaism as mainly a religion, while more than half consider their Jewishness a matter of ancestry (fifty-two percent) or culture (fifty-five percent).[1] Jews know that they might pray three times a day or they might be atheists – and they can still be Jewish. So, can we still call Judaism a "religion"?

Meanwhile, in Russia, when asked to fill out their citizenship papers, Russian Jews are forced to write "Jewish" in the box asking for nationality. Not Russian, but Jewish. Yet we know today Jews can have different color skin, come from different countries, speak different languages, eat different traditional foods, and they can still be Jewish. Jews are a multi-racial, multi-ethnic people with all types of backgrounds from any nation in the world. So, can we really call it a "nationality"?

At the same time, Judaism has to be more than bagels and Mel Brooks – and not only because these are elements of the "Ashkenormative" Jewish culture, but because it has to be more than just food and comedy and movies and Yiddish. Sephardic Jews and Indian Jews and Asian Jews have their own unique Jewish culture, as well. In which case, "culture" isn't the right word to describe Judaism either, right?

According to Rabbi Mordecai Kaplan, who was addressing this topic over a hundred years ago, as he wrote in his famous book *Judaism as a Civilization*, Jews can be Jewish through one of three Bs:

1. Believing – believing in the things that Jews are supposed to believe in (as opposed to other faith systems).

2. Behaving – doing the things that Jews are supposed to do, like keep the Sabbath, pray a certain way, or eat only kosher food.

---

1. "Jewish Americans in 2020," Pew Research Center, Washington, D.C., May 2021, https://www.pewforum.org/2021/05/11/jewish-identity-and-belief/ .HYPERLINK "" .

3. Belonging – being an automatic part of this group called the Jewish People with a shared history and a shared destiny simply by having been born to Jewish ancestors.

Avraham Infeld, when he was president of Hillel International, used to ask young people around the world to do this exercise. He'd show them a poster board with apples, bananas, and oranges, and he'd ask them to put "Jew" alongside two other words in the same family. What he found most interesting were not the answers the students gave, but that the answers varied from country to country.

For instance, in the US, they would write: "Protestants, Catholics, Muslims." But in Israel they would add "Arabs" to the list, and Russians would invariably include, "Russians" and maybe "Georgians," as well. Meanwhile, Infeld says the Latin Americans were the most unpredictable and would usually claim, "there is nothing comparable" to being Jewish.[2]

This is why many of us prefer to define Jews as a People rather than any of those other insufficient descriptors. We talk of Jewish Peoplehood to describe the commitment we have to each other, but what is Jewish Peoplehood exactly? This is how the Center for Jewish Peoplehood Education defines it:

> Jewish Peoplehood – the state of being part of the Jewish People – is first and foremost *a sense of belonging to the Jewish collective*. We understand this sense of belonging as much more than a simplistic, emotional connection to the Jewish collective. Rather,

---

2. Avraham Infeld, *A Passion for A People: Lessons from the Life of a Jewish Educator* (Jerusalem: Melitz, 2017), 36.

it reflects a deep identification with a collective consciousness that is a product of the long, rich, historical journey of the Jewish People.

That collective consciousness is composed of a shared past – a covenant of fate – and a shared future – a covenant of destiny. Being part of the Jewish People offers every Jew the ownership, as a member in the collective, of the Jewish People's assets accumulated throughout history, be it Jewish texts, Jewish values, practices, languages or Jewish civilization in its various manifestations.

It also entails responsibility for the future of the Jewish people and Jewish civilization. Peoplehood is a consciousness assumed by individuals by virtue of their membership in the collective. It shapes their identity, the way they perceive the world and how they act on their perceptions. It is a worldview whose core values are the thriving of the Jewish people, its collective enterprise and its contribution to humanity.[3]

While Jewish Peoplehood helps shape one's identity, Jewish identity has evolved over time and continues to evolve. Let's take something as inconsequential as clothing as an example. Clothing, of course, is a definitive part of one's culture. Dressing a particular way allows others to identify you as a part of a specific tribe. But what would you say is the Jewish way

---

3. "Conceptual: What Is Peoplehood?" *The Center for Jewish Peoplehood Education,* published June 26, 2013, https://jpeoplehood.org/toolkit/what-why-how/conceptual/#What_is_Jewish_Peoplehood.

to dress? What would constitute Jewish clothing? And has it remained static over time?

If you've ever seen images of the Rambam (Maimonides), who lived in Spain in the twelfth century and is accepted by all Jews to have been one of the greatest Jewish scholars to ever live, you'll notice that he wore a turban and long robes. But is that how the Baal Shem Tov, the father of Chasidic Judaism, dressed in Poland in the eighteenth century? Is that how the early Zionist pioneers in Palestine dressed in the early twentieth century? Is that how modern Orthodox Jews dress today? Is that how secular Jews dress?

My point in sharing that simple example is to show that Judaism has evolved over the centuries to adapt to modern life, and I believe Jewish identity is evolving yet again, into its fourth iteration, what I call "Jewish Peoplehood 4.0."

But let's start at the beginning, shall we? Let's start with Jewish Peoplehood 1.0.[4]

Jewish Peoplehood 1.0

Judaism began with Abraham. According to the Bible, Abraham was the first Jew. He married Sarah and they had a son, Isaac. Isaac married Rebecca and they had twin sons, Jacob and Esau. Jacob married both Leah and Rachel and had twelve sons. Abraham, Isaac and Jacob are affectionately known as

---

4. Disclaimer: Please note that I've attempted to capture over three thousand years of Jewish history in a few short pages. This is not intended to be a thorough retelling of the Jewish past. There are many excellent resources if one would like to explore the Jewish story in more depth. This thumbnail sketch is meant to provide a broad overview for the purpose of capturing the evolution of Judaism into three main eras.

the "patriarchs" in Jewish tradition, while the "matriarchs" are, classically, Sarah, Rebecca, Rachel, and Leah. Jacob became known as "Israel," which means "to wrestle with God" and is a very appropriate description of the Jewish People, and hence, the Jewish People are also known as the Children of Israel. Jacob's aforementioned twelve sons became the twelve tribes of Israel, and his favored son, Joseph, after some rough roads, wound up in Egypt as advisor to the Pharaoh. Eventually, all of the Israelites went down to Egypt because of a famine in the land of Israel.

While in Egypt, the Jews multiplied and grew wealthy, until a new Pharaoh came to power who didn't know Joseph and enslaved the Israelites. Then, according to the tradition, Moses freed the Israelites from slavery – which was no small task, of course – and brought them to Mt. Sinai where they received the Ten Commandments from God, which is when Judaism began to have laws, regulations, decision-making structures, etc.

Moses led the Jews through forty years of wandering in the desert. During that time, Judaism was in a wandering phase. Our spirituality traveled with us. God traveled with us. And we had a portable Holy Ark housed in a tent called the *Mishkan.* (Remember *Raiders of the Lost Ark?* That was the Holy Ark in the *Mishkan.*) This was Judaism 1.0 – the Judaism of Wandering.

During this period, Judaism was defined by all three of Kaplan's B's: Believing, Behaving, and Belonging. Jews were expected to believe in the one true God, as instructed in the first two of the Ten Commandments. (The first is, "I am the Lord your God," while the second is, "You shall have no other gods before Me.")[5]) They were expected to behave a certain way, as instructed by the rest of the commandments, along with other rules and regulations provided by God in the written Torah. And they belonged to the Jewish People simply by virtue of saying they belonged. I'll share two quick stories to explain what that means.

According to the Bible, Moses married a Cushite woman whose parents were not Jewish, but she was accepted as one of the Jewish people. In fact, when Miriam and Aaron – Moses's sister and brother – criticized Moses's choice, God punished them for speaking ill of Moses, but God didn't actually punish Moses for his choice in a wife.[6]

In the Book of Ruth, after Ruth's husband died, she said to her mother-in-law, Naomi, who was Jewish, "For wherever you go, I will go; where you lodge, I will lodge; your people shall be my people, and your God my God."[7] This statement was enough to make Ruth, who was not born Jewish, officially part of the Jewish People. It's worth noting that King David – one of Judaism's most revered leaders – was Ruth's grandson, and it is believed that the future Messiah will come from David's line. So, it all started with Ruth, who converted to Judaism by making that one simple statement.

I share these two stories of examples of how belonging is such a key component of being Jewish during Judaism 1.0, as well as how easy it was to become a member of the Jewish people back then. You just had to say, "I'm in!"

Eventually, Moses led the Jewish People back to the

---

5.   Exodus 20:2.
6.   Numbers 12:1-10.
7.   Ruth 1:16.

Promised Land, to the Land of Israel. Though he himself was not able to lead them into Israel, his successor, Joshua, did so. And that was the beginning of the transition to the Jews becoming a stationary people, a people with a permanent home.

Jewish Peoplehood 2.0

When the Jews finally resettled in Israel, around the year 1270 BCE under the leadership of Joshua after succeeding Moses, they underwent another period of transition. They had a home, but they had not yet built the Holy Temple. After three hundred years in the Holy Land, the Holy Temple was built in the tenth century BCE. That officially marked the next phase in Judaism.

This was the Judaism of having a home and a center. Our holiness went from being portable to being stationary. The Jews had our own land, with a thriving, singular community. The Temple became the center of our Jewish life. That was the first upgrade in our Operating System from 1.0 to 2.0.

During this period, Jews were not expected to live only in Israel, but they were expected to make pilgrimage three times a year to Jerusalem, specifically to the Holy Temple. The Temple was where Jews would bring sacrifices and honor God. Jewish life was about how to live a moral life, how to mark time with rituals, how to celebrate holidays, how to live a structured day, week, month, year – indeed, an entire life – and how to honor God, and the Temple was at the center of it.

Then in 586 BCE, the Temple was destroyed – the first time. About seventy years later, it was rebuilt. Then, the Second Temple was destroyed in the year 70 CE. When the Second Temple was destroyed, the Jews were thrown out of

Jerusalem by the Romans. Despite a valiantly fought rebellion, with the destruction of the Temple, most of that form of Judaism was completely crushed. Some elements have continued, including marking time with those central holidays and rituals like Shabbat, but even many of the holidays evolved in their symbolism and how they were celebrated. That is when Judaism began to undergo its second major transformation.

Jewish Peoplehood 3.0

After the destruction of the Second Temple, we became a dispersed community. Most of the Jews were exiled, and that was the beginning of Judaism 3.0 – the Judaism of the Diaspora. Without animal sacrifice and the high priesthood, Judaism had to change. New leaders and scholars emerged who captured our stories, wrote down the Oral Law (the Mishnah) so it could go hand-in-hand with the Written Law (the Torah) and would not be lost to the future generations.

These leaders, called rabbis, codified a system of law – called the *halachah* – which became the defining feature of Judaism. We created synagogues where we could pray instead of offering animal sacrifices, and we built schools where scholars of the law could lead the community in learning. Believe it or not, this is pretty much still the Judaism we see today.

In the third century CE, the Mishnah, which was the Oral Law passed down through the generations, was compiled by Yehuda Hanassi. Then the study of the Talmud, which is the Mishnah along with the Gemara, commentary from the greatest scholars over generations, became the center of Jewish culture for over 1,500 years. Of course, rabbis differed as to how to interpret the laws and stories, and different schools of thought developed around the greatest of the rabbis, but Torah and Talmud study was central to Judaism during this time.

As a sidebar, the Talmud was the original interconnected document. It allowed for multiple commentators over many generations to engage with what was written and offer their own interpretations – all written down in one place with a vibrant back-and-forth. Think about the most important, relevant, incisive essay you've read on the internet and then picture the comments that come at the bottom of the article – at least, think about the articulate, respectful, challenging, non-anonymous ones – and that is the Talmud, only written 1,800 years ago!

Despite these differences between Jewish Peoplehood 2.0 and 3.0, being Jewish was still defined by Kaplan's three Bs. Jews must behave a certain way, based on the rules of the *halachah*. Jews must believe a certain way, based on God's commandments in the Torah. And Jews must belong to the group, by having been born to a Jewish mother. Non-Jews could still convert to Judaism, but the process became more complicated than in Ruth's day. And if you didn't embrace all three Bs, then the Jewish community could disown you.

Cracks in Jewish Peoplehood 3.0

Influenced by the secularization of European society during the Enlightenment, life started to change for the Jews, too. Jews began to do Jewish differently. We became integrated into the societies where we lived. Jews had tried this before – during the Hellenization period and the Golden Age of Spain, as two examples – but with less success. Now, carving out our

Jewish identity as something separate from religious faith was having more success. Jews started becoming involved in the scientific, philosophical, and artistic thinking of the greater society around them. Slowly but surely, Jewish identity was starting to shift.

The Enlightenment was referred to by the Jews as the Haskalah ("Enlightenment" in Hebrew), and it was epitomized by challenges to tradition. The eighteenth-century Jewish philosopher Moses Mendelssohn, himself observant, challenged the norms that defined religious belief and practice, especially in Judaism. His work was revolutionary and it drew the praise of transformational philosophers of the time, like Immanuel Kant.

The Emancipation led to Jews being accepted as citizens in many of the countries where they lived. They were no longer being forced to live in ghettos and wear clothing that marked them as different. This acceptance led to an earthquake in Jewish Peoplehood 3.0 – the birth of Reform Judaism in the early 1800s. The idea was to make Judaism into a system of belief that reflected modern times, while holding on to some eternal truths so the practitioner could choose which elements to incorporate into his or her life. German Reform synagogues changed their practices to emulate Christian society. They added more German language to the service, introduced choirs and organs to provide music, and allowed mixed seating of men and women.

This Jewish Reformation was exported to America, where the first Reform synagogue, Kahal Kadosh Beth Elohim, was founded in South Carolina in the mid-1800s. By 1880, ninety percent of American synagogues were Reform.[8] In 1886, a year after the Reform movement adopted the Pittsburgh Platform, the Conservative movement was born as an attempt to bridge Reform Judaism with tradition.[9]

During the early 1900s, as Jewish immigration to America exploded with Jews fleeing the antisemitism of the Old World, these new American Jews lived together in cities and towns, building their own synagogues, social welfare organizations, Jewish community centers, and schools. The immigrant generation generally spoke the Old World languages among themselves but taught their children English, as they strove to make the first generation American Jewish kids into "real Americans," including giving their children Americanized names.

It's been said that the Jewish Community Center movement, which began in 1917, was started to teach Jews how to be Americans, whereas today, over one hundred years later, JCCs exist to teach Americans how to be Jewish. Mark Sokoll, CEO of the JCCs of Greater Boston, said, "Our grandparents came to the JCC because they were Jewish. But our grandchildren will be Jewish because they came to the JCC."

The Jews in America spent the first half of the twentieth century trying desperately to be accepted by the larger society, but it wasn't easy. In many ways they were still seen as second-class citizens. Universities had quotas on the number

---

8. "Reform Judaism: The Tenets of Reform Judaism," *Jewish Virtual Library*, accessed January 17, 2021,
   https://www.jewishvirtuallibrary.org/the-tenets-of-reform-judaism
9. "Conservative Judaism: How the Middle Became a Movement," *My Jewish Learning*, last modified December 7, 2017, https://www.myjewishlearning.com/article/conservative-judaism-how-the-middle-became-a-movement/

of Jews they would accept. Many country clubs would not allow Jews to join. Some cities in America wouldn't even allow Jews to own land.[10]

So, as much as the Jews of the twentieth century wanted to turn their Judaism into just a religion, the world around them wouldn't allow them to. In fact, as American Jews were struggling with second-class status, in parts of the Arab world and in Europe it was much worse. Pogroms and state-sponsored antisemitism were a regular occurrence there. In fact, the Dreyfus affair in France, in which a Jewish military officer was falsely accused of treason, was one noteworthy example of state-sponsored antisemitism because it led to the formation of the modern political Zionist movement by Theodore Herzl, which highlighted the need for Jews to have their own independent state in the land of Israel, where pioneering Jews had already been laboring to settle the land for nearly one hundred years.

Of course, Nazism was on the rise too, which defined Jews as a race. The Nuremberg Laws dictated that only one Jewish grandparent made a person a Jew. One's beliefs, practices, even conversion to Christianity didn't matter. As long as a person had "Jewish blood," they were still a Jew.

During the unfathomable tragedy of the Holocaust, two thirds of European Jewry were murdered. Then in 1948, Israel was officially recognized as a state and Israel's first law, the Basic Law, was passed, granting any Jew anywhere in the

---

10. Sharon Waxman, "Judgment at Pasadena: The Nuremberg Laws Were in California Since 1945. Who Knew?" *Washington Post*, March 16, 2000, https://www.washingtonpost.com/wp-srv/WPcap/2000-03/16/076r-031600-idx.html.

world the right to move to Israel to claim citizenship there. The concept of this was to provide a safe haven for Jews facing persecution around the world so that what had happened in Europe would not happen again. The law was later refined to reflect the Nuremberg definition of who is a Jew: most people with at least one Jewish grandparent can move to Israel and claim citizenship as a Jew.[11]

Of course, the rebirth of Israel has led to the reintroduction of the idea of Judaism as a nationality. And to make it more complicated, Israeli Jews seem to have a culture uniquely differing from that of Diaspora Jews too, with their own food, their own sense of humor, a language not known by most Diaspora Jews, and even their own notion of religiosity. Oh, and Israeli culture is not monolithic either, as Mizrachi Jews (Jews from the Middle East and North Africa) have quite different customs, for example, from Ashkenazi Israelis.

So now, this Jewish evolution that began with the Enlightenment is coming to a head. Now, Jewish Peoplehood is reaching its next inflection point. Enough momentum has built up around the cognitive dissonance that Jews are experiencing what Rabbi Benay Lappe, the founder of Svara, calls "a sociological crash."[12]

---

11. The ministry that oversees religion in Israel has a different definition of who is a Jew, insisting that only someone born to a certifiably Jewish mother is actually Jewish. This conflict between the two competing definitions of who is a Jew in Israel – the definition provided by the Ministry of Religion and the one given by the Ministry of Absorption – has led to deep tension between Israel and Diaspora Judaism. More on this in the next chapter.
12. Benay Lappe, "CRASH! 1-2-3 How to Navigate Inevitable Change," filmed January 2014 at TEDxSpenceSchool, New York, video, 18:42, https://www.youtube.com/watch?v=WTdeIFK7VSc.

According to Rabbi Lappe, when someone's worldview is challenged by new facts on the ground, they experience a "crash." Everything they believed is called into question. The foundation for their system of seeing the world has been upended. It's a major psychological event with significant consequences. According to Lappe, when people experience this crash, they can react in one of three ways:

1. They can double down. They can build walls around their rituals, practices, and old ways of thinking and push out the alternative views. This is what the extreme zealots do. Today, in the twenty-first century, religious zealots prohibit access to TV, the internet, mainstream magazines and newspapers, and in fact much of the outside world.

2. The next option is for them to walk away from the old way all together. They not only drop the old worldview, but they completely embrace the new one. Often this is what happens when believers become atheists. For example, there is a story in the Talmud about Rabbi Elisha ben Avuyah, who completely walks away from God and Judaism because, according to one account, he watches a child die immediately after the child conscientiously observes God's commandments.[13]

3. The third alternative is to innovate, to try to combine the old worldview with the new evidence. We see this today with many Jews embracing Eastern practices like mediation and yoga. We see this in the creative solutions to Shabbat observance when new technology is invented, like the Shabbat elevators that travel without needing anyone to push a button.

Embracing this third way is what has allowed Jews to survive

---

13. Talmud, *Kiddushin* 39b.

for over three thousand years. Our ability to adapt, acculturate, and assimilate has ensured that we can keep on keeping on. The key has been not losing ourselves completely to the nations and cultures that absorb us, holding on to certain central elements of our Judaism, and always holding on to our Jewish soul.

Shabbat, for example, is a central element of our Jewish Peoplehood and, hence, our Jewish soul. Ahad Ha'am, the founder of Cultural Zionism, famously said, "More than the Jews have kept Shabbat, Shabbat has kept the Jews." (More on Shabbat in chapter five.) But what else is central to Judaism? What other elements have kept this tradition alive for thousands of years? What elements will ensure that Judaism lives on for another thousand years? And what, if anything, is that central core element that makes all of us Jewish, no matter what we look like, sound like, practice, or believe?

Entrepreneur and social activist Tal Keinan believes if we don't answer these questions right now, we risk the very future of Judaism. In his book *God Is in the Crowd*, he writes the following:

> If the Jewish People is to survive, in Israel, in the United States, and in the remnants of Diaspora, Judaism must reclaim its relevance to the individual by reestablishing its spiritual value. It must reclaim its relevance to the community by finding common cause among a critical mass of its individual adherents. This can happen only through the continued evolution of Jewish thought and practice. In an era of seemingly

limitless personal options, our choice as a community is stark: Create meaning in Judaism or accept extinction.[14]

A Story of Transition

In the next chapter, I will lay out five meta-trends that I believe have led us to this moment. But I want to end this chapter with a story of the last crash, the last time our Jewish Operating System evolved from 2.0 to 3.0. I want to take us back to the year 70 CE.

Seventy years after Jesus was born, Rome attacked Jerusalem. And by attacking, I mean leveling the place. Jerusalem was being burned to the ground. The Jewish zealots who were leading the defense against the Roman attack declared that this was a fight to the death. They said that no one was allowed to leave the city of Jerusalem – unless they were in a coffin.

But one man, a visionary named Yohanan Ben Zakkai, realized that if Jerusalem fell, and the Holy Temple was destroyed, and no one escaped, then Judaism as they knew it could become extinct. No survivors would mean no passing on Jewish life for the future. So, he came up with a plan to sneak out of Jerusalem – by faking his own death. He had his students build him a coffin and carry him out of the city as if he were actually dead.

The ruse worked. Ben Zakkai's students snuck him out of the city, and they brought the coffin to the tent of the Roman

---

14. Tal Keinan, *God Is in the Crowd* (New York: Spiegel & Grau, 2018), xi.

general, Vespasian. When they set down the coffin, Ben Zakkai popped out and hailed Vespasian as caesar.

Vespasian, no doubt a bit surprised, challenged Ben Zakkai: "I'm not Caeser. Caesar is back in Rome." But at that very moment, a messenger from Rome arrived to tell Vespasian that Caesar had been killed and now he, Vespasian, was the new caesar.

Vespasian turned to Ben Zakkai, moved by the man's prophecy, and he asked Ben Zakkai what he wanted. Ben Zakkai didn't ask for power or money. Instead, he asked to be put in charge of a school called Yavneh where Jewish students studied. He famously said, "Give me Yavneh and its sages." Vespasian obliged, and it was at that school where Ben Zakkai and his students created the future of Jewish life.[15]

At that moment, Judaism began to evolve for its second time, so that it could be relevant and meaningful in a time when the Jews were dispersed from Jerusalem, when the Holy Temple was destroyed and Judaism could no longer be what it was. Yohanan Ben Zakkai began a religious revolution. The Temple evolved into synagogues, the priests transitioned into rabbis, animal sacrifice became prayer, and the study of our sacred texts became central to what it means to practice Judaism in a post-Temple period.

This is the Judaism we've been practicing for the last two thousand years. But what will be the Judaism we practice for the next two thousand years? Are we on the eve of another religious revolution? And if we are, how can we make Jewish

---

15. Talmud, *Gittin* 56a–b.

life meaningful, relevant, and joyous for the future? Andrés Spokoiny, CEO of the Jewish Funders Network, wrote:

> To be sure, our Jewish spiritual software was overdue for an update well before COVID19.... Our theological and philosophical frameworks, the ideological scaffolding of Jewish life, is still based on nineteenth- and twentieth-century ideologies. Reform, Conservative, Orthodox, ultra-Orthodox, and Zionist approaches are all *responses* to the realities of the Jewish people in past centuries. They are all products of the clash between traditional Judaism and the revolutionary conditions of modernity.[16]

Isn't it time to adapt the "ideological scaffolding of Jewish life" to the next evolution in Jewish Peoplehood?

---

16. Andrés Spokoiny, "The Future of Jewish Communal Life," *Tablet*, July 10, 2020, https://www.tabletmag.com/sections/community/articles/communal-life-after-pandemic.

3

Not Your Bubby's Judaism: Five Meta-Trends Driving Change

Several years ago, a friend was diagnosed with breast cancer. She was only in her twenties, engaged to be married and in the prime of her life. Obviously, this news devastated her, but fortunately, the doctors caught it early enough that intervention was going to work. And it did.

The medical experts did what they needed to do and between radiation, surgery, and chemotherapy, they put her breast cancer into remission. Unfortunately, the spiritual experts didn't do their job quite as well.

During her diagnosis and subsequent treatment, my friend sought answers to all sorts of questions – mostly the spiritual type. She was not a regular synagogue-goer, but exceptional circumstances call for exceptional measures, so she went to her rabbi for advice. The rabbi provided some guidance and invited her to come back for services during Shabbat, where the entire congregation could offer her and her family a "*Mi She'berach*," the traditional prayer of healing.

So the next Saturday, she came to services. When it was time for the congregation to give their communal blessing for a "*refuah shelemah*" (a speedy recovery), they invited her and her family onto the *bimah* (the stage at the front of the congregation). She approached the *bimah* with her fiancé, and when asked for their Hebrew names, her fiancé told the rabbi that he wasn't Jewish. At that point, the rabbi asked him to step off the *bimah*.

As you can imagine, my friend was shocked and embarrassed. Was this the Judaism she believed in? Was this the Judaism she wanted to continue to practice? Was this the Judaism she wanted to raise her family with? Absolutely not.

Fortunately, the cancer was cured. However, her relationship to her Jewishness did not heal quite so well.

It's complicated to be Jewish. In the words of Tevye from *Fiddler on the Roof*, "Sometimes I wonder, when it gets too quiet up there, if You [God] are thinking, 'What kind of mischief can I play on my friend, Tevye?'"

Like Tevye's daughter, my friend married a non-Jew. And in the movie, Tevye's daughter is cast aside, shunned and pushed out of the Jewish community. Tevye tears his clothing to represent that his daughter had actually died in his eyes for this heretical act.

My friend, on the other hand, while made to feel unwelcome by the rabbi at that specific synagogue, was not exiled by her Jewish community. In fact, many years later, I saw her, her husband, and their two kids celebrating at a Rosh Hashanah service in the park. It took a while, but ultimately, she came back to her Jewishness – albeit to a different rabbi!

Whether we like it or not, Judaism is evolving. Jews are becoming fully accepted by many societies in the Diaspora – societies that are majority non-Jewish. With that acceptance, Jews are acculturating and assimilating.

It's possible that Jews will either evolve away from

Judaism – finding a new path, a non-Jewish path – or they will pull Judaism along with them, forcing Judaism to evolve – like it has several times before.

This is what leads me to believe we are on the cusp of evolving to the next phase, Jewish Peoplehood 4.0. As I said in the last chapter, a few hundred years ago, if you were Jewish, it defined everything about you: where you lived, how you dressed, what you ate, whom you married, how you lived your days and weeks, what you did for a living, etc. But today, if you are Jewish, it is only one piece of your identity.

In the twenty-first century, non-traditional Jews have multiple identities. You might be a student and a soccer player, a New Yorker and a sorority sister, a dancer and a volunteer, and somewhere in there, you might also be Jewish.

But today, it's not enough to *be* Jewish. You also have to consciously choose to do Jewish. If your Jewishness is just one piece of your identity, what is going to make it important enough for you to choose it over other pieces of your identity? What is going to make it relevant enough to be accessed regularly? Will it be the part of you that marks time – the days of the week, the weeks of the month, the months of the year? Will it be the part of you that helps you decide how you eat? Will it be the part of you that helps determine your worldview, your politics, and the way you engage with your neighbors?

Regardless of how we choose to do Jewish today, the likelihood is that we are making a choice that looks different from how our grandparents chose to do Jewish. And I'd be willing to bet quite a few shekels that our kids will not choose to do Jewish the way our parents did. In fact, I'd wager that the old ways of doing Jewish won't work at all in the future for most Jews. We can't just keep doing what we did a hundred years ago and expecting it to work. And frankly, if we keep trying to, then we will be lucky if our grandkids do Jewish at all!

We must find new ways to inspire the next generation to see their Jewish identity as something they couldn't possible live without. Which means we could be on the eve of a new era in Jewish Peoplehood. This could be a moment in time when doing Jewish will begin to look very different than it used to look. This unique moment in our history could be transformative.

Why now? What's different about this moment? I believe there are five overarching drivers, or meta-trends, forcing the evolution of Jewish Peoplehood to the next stage. Let's take them one at a time.

Dropping Institutional Affiliation

I used to sit on the board of a Conservative synagogue. As board members, we were all responsible for attending services at least once every two months to be an usher and welcome worshippers into services on Saturday mornings. For some, this was easy and natural, since they were regulars at Shabbat services on Saturday mornings. For others, like me, this was not the way I'd ordinarily spend a Saturday morning, so it was definitely a forced obligation. Nevertheless, I took it seriously and I fulfilled my obligation.

One particular Saturday morning, my eldest Talia, who was only five years old at the time, asked to go with me. I was pleasantly surprised, as she hadn't asked to join me ever before. I was also wary that she'd be bored, so I brought some items to keep her busy during the three-hour services. To my delight, she paid attention for the better part of a half hour.

Then, as she began to squirm, I encouraged her to find something fun to do. So, she dipped into the bag of distractions and pulled out a coloring book.

With a smile on her face, she began coloring quietly, minding her own business. After only a couple minutes, however, one of the other ushers came up to her and scolded her in a harsh whisper. The woman wagged a finger at her and hissed into her face, "You can't write on Shabbat. You're desecrating this space and the Sabbath."

As I moved quickly across the sanctuary to intervene, the other usher roughly pulled the book and crayons out of her hands. My daughter was devastated – and confused. Had she done something wrong? Was she in trouble? Why was this woman so upset with her?

I was irate. This was no way to create a warm, welcoming space. This was no way to attract congregants. Hell, this was no way to treat a child! And I let this usher know exactly how I felt.

Later, I let the rabbi know how I felt too. He sympathized, and apologized on behalf of the congregation, agreeing that the over-zealous usher had acted inappropriately. Nevertheless, my daughter never wanted to go with me to services again. And I didn't sit on that board for much longer, either.

It doesn't take an incident like that to drive most modern, untraditional Jews away from synagogue life. For some, the synagogue service doesn't speak to them. For others, they're not interested in all the baggage associated with a synagogue. And for most, they just have more interesting things to do on Saturday mornings. The bottom line is that Jews are not affiliating with legacy institutions the way they used to.

According to the Pew survey of 2020 on American Jews,

only thirty-five percent say someone in their household is a member of a synagogue.[1] Even fewer actively participate in synagogue services, with only twenty percent of Jewish adults saying "they attend services at a synagogue, temple, minyan or havurah at least once a month."[2]

Surely traditional Jews will always seek a more traditional space for their worship. However, the majority of the next generation of non-traditional Jews are searching for sacred spaces that look different – spaces that are welcoming to children, that embrace nature, that have more gender parity in their leadership, that speak to their quest for spirituality more than dogma.

There are a handful of independent *minyanim*[3] in the US that understand this and have capitalized on this trend. In his book *Empowered Judaism*, Rabbi Elie Kaunfer says,

> The future of Jewish life is dependent on Jews – not just rabbis – taking hold of the rich, challenging, surprising, and inspiring heritage that makes up our texts and traditions.... The independent *minyanim* are a great example of this vision in action, but they are just one example.[4]

---

1. "Jewish Americans in 2020," Pew Research Center, Washington, D.C., May 2021, https://www.pewforum.org/2021/05/11/jewish-identity-and-belief/.
2. "Jewish Americans in 2020," Pew Research Center, Washington, D.C., May 2021, https://www.pewforum.org/2021/05/11/jewish-americans-in-2020/.
3. Independent *minyanim* are prayer and study communities that exist independently from the established denominations (Orthodox, Conservative, Reform, and Reconstructionist) and don't conform to traditional synagogue structures.
4. Elie Kaunfer, *Empowered Judaism: What Independent Minyanim Can Teach Us about Building Vibrant Jewish Communities* (Woodstock, VT: Jewish Lights, 2010), 1.

These independent *minyanim* are some of the fastest growing congregations in America, in part because they are led by young, charismatic leaders, they don't conform to the old standards, and they are not beholden to anachronistic membership models. Congregations like IKAR in Los Angeles, The Kitchen in San Francisco, Mishkan in Chicago and Lab/Shul in New York are thriving, while many of the traditional institutions are struggling to pay their bills.

Synagogues are not the only institutions with lagging affiliation. The Jewish Community Federations of North America, which have traditionally been American Jews' central address for organized umbrella giving to Jewish causes, have seen a major drop in donations over the last quarter century. According to one study, "giving to Jewish federations has dropped nearly thirty-eight percent in inflation-adjusted dollars over the past twenty-five years."[5]

Either modern Jews are opting out of all Jewish affiliations or they are creating their own, new outlets. While some leaders, particularly synagogue rabbis, may call this a crisis, others like David Bryfman from the Jewish Education Project, say it's our greatest success. He told me the fact that young people want to opt in to do Jewish their own way doesn't mean we have failed, but that in fact we have succeeded. He said, "We've made them want to be Jewish *and* be free thinkers."

Over the last decade, organizations like UpStart have helped give birth to over 1,450 initiatives and trained more

---

5.   Josh Nathan Kazis, "Why Are Jewish Federations Struggling With Fundraising as Charitable Giving by Americans Hits Record?" *Forward*, June 15, 2016, https://forward.com/news/342720/why-are-jewish-federations-struggling-with-fundraising-as-charitable-giving/.

than 3,200 up-and-coming Jewish leaders. *Slingshot*, an annual publication of the most innovative programs and projects in the Jewish world, has highlighted hundreds of unique projects since the year 2005. Dan Libenson and Lex Rofeberg, the hosts of the *Judaism Unbound* podcast, which has reached over one million downloads, have interviewed hundreds of thought leaders who are changing the way we think about Judaism.

While risky ideas and bold initiatives in the Jewish world are exciting – indeed, they will be the lifeblood of the Jewish future – this is not a new phenomenon. We remake ourselves in every generation. We tweak, we reform, we iterate. In the end, we wind up with something that is more relevant for a new generation.

What is different now is the fact that most legacy institutions (meaning synagogues and hundred-year-old Jewish institutions) are not attracting new members and donors the way they used to. This will have enormous ramifications for how Jews think about community, centralized decision making, and philanthropy. For example, if the next generation of Jews decides to only support programs they personally use or benefit from, what will that mean for the future of less-often-used programs? Surely, they will disappear. While some will say this is a good thing – that we should let the market decide what lives and what dies and allow those projects that are less relevant to fade away – it could mean the end of under-funded services that still provide a vital role but are less appealing.

One example that comes to mind is the need for Jewish funeral services. Young Jews surely don't think about supporting the *chevra kadisha* (Jewish burial society) when they are young. But if they will choose to have a Jewish burial one day, then they'll need the *chevra kadisha*. Who will support it in the interim? Who will keep it alive and healthy? Just as you can't buy an insurance policy the day you need it, the same goes for institutions funded by philanthropy.

The benefit of the big umbrella institutions is that they fund the full spectrum of community services. They ensure dollars are sprinkled around to make sure even the less popular recipients can stay in business for that day when they are needed. But with directed giving taking over philanthropy, and donors only wanting to give to their pet projects, what will happen to the umbrella organizations? Could that mean the age of the big institution is over?

Shifting Jewish Ethnography

The second factor that is leading to an evolution in the Jewish operating system has to do with shifting ethnicity and demographics within Judaism. Together, these make up our shifting ethnography.

A Japanese woman who sits on the board of directors of the Oshman Family JCC in Palo Alto likes to call herself "the Japanese *shiksa*." Her husband is Jewish, but he's not the one ensuring their family continues to do Jewish. And while she didn't convert, she is lighting Shabbat candles with her children, making Passover Seder for her family, and schlepping the kids to Hebrew school. So, you tell me – is she really not a Jewish member of that family?

In the absence of ethnicity as a de facto determining factor of Jewishness, what are the new foundations of Jewishness? What challenges do we face?

Ashkenazi and Sephardi Jews no longer have the

monopoly on the market they thought they used to have, as we have embraced Korean Jews, Indian Jews, African American Jews, etc. Maternal descent no longer rules the day as the accepted definition of "who is a Jew." Interfaith marriage is a foregone conclusion. Today, even non-Jewish Jews are active in our communities – meaning those who have taken upon themselves all the trappings of living a Jewish life, but haven't officially converted.

Rabbi Angela Buchdahl of Central Synagogue in New York was the first woman to lead the synagogue in its 180-year history. That is a long-overdue accomplishment, to be sure. But even more surprising is that she is the first Asian American to be ordained as a rabbi in the US.[6] The Jews of Color Initiative was founded only recently to focus on "building and advancing the professional, organizational and communal field for Jews of Color," according to the mission page on their website. But Be'chol Lashon was founded in 2000 to raise "awareness about ethnic, racial, and cultural diversity of Jewish identity and experience."[7] These are all signs that we are moving quickly to embrace this ethnographic shift.

Let's take intermarriage as another example of this shift. For generations, the Jewish community has felt the greatest threat to its survival is intermarriage – too many Jews marrying non-Jews. According to the most recent Pew survey of 2020, "If one excludes the Orthodox and looks only at

---

6.   Yair Ettinger, "'Judaism Shouldn't Have to Stay Alive Only Because Jews Are Afraid of Everything Else,'" *Haaretz*, January 14, 2019, https://www.haaretz.com/us-news/1.6828507.

7.   https://globaljews.org/about/mission/.

non-Orthodox Jews who have gotten married since 2010, seventy-two percent are intermarried.[8]

I understand the worry of the traditionalists. They'll argue that when a kid is faced with a choice of Hanukkah or Christmas, in America the pressure to choose Christmas is so overwhelming that of course they'll choose Christmas. And when given the opportunity to celebrate both, then why not?! From there, the fear is that it's a slippery slope to giving up Judaism all together.

In fact, the data shows that after a Jew marries a non-Jew, there is an even greater chance that their children will be less Jewish and more likely to marry a non-Jew. According to the same Pew survey, eighty-two percent of Jews who only have one Jewish parent are likely to marry a non-Jew.[9]

Nevertheless, even according to strict traditionalists, a third generation of children – if descended from a Jewish mother and a Jewish grandmother – is still Jewish. So, what are we to make of this shifting ethnography?

In 2012, the Jim Joseph Foundation created a plan to invest money in ten different communities around the US to build new teen programs. By 2014, nine were funded and launched but the tenth had not yet been funded. That was because the Foundation wanted the Bay Area, where they are based, to be one of the recipients and the community hadn't gotten its act together yet.

So, the Jewish Community Federation of San Francisco partnered with some local organizations, including the OFJCC

---

8. "Jewish Americans in 2020," Pew Research Center, Washington, D.C. May 2021, https://www.pewforum.org/2021/05/11/marriage-families-and-children/.
9. ""Jewish Americans in 2020," Pew Research Center, Washington, D.C. May 2021, https://www.pewforum.org/2021/05/11/marriage-families-and-children/.

in Palo Alto, to do focus groups, gather data, and determine what kind of teen program the teens wanted. It turns out Northern California teens were unique in several ways. The most striking result of the research was that teens in the Bay Area overwhelmingly wanted to be able to bring their non-Jewish friends to their Jewish programs. It turns out they are proud of their Jewishness and they want to share it, but they also feel uncomfortable in spaces that are not open to their non-Jewish friends.

This conflict of particularism (or tribalism) versus universalism is deep and profound amongst millennials and Gen Zers. Young people are very uncomfortable with the idea that choosing their Jewish friends or groups over non-Jewish friends or groups makes them somehow exclusionary or even racist.

In 2017, I was invited to speak to the young leadership group of the 92nd Street Y in New York about the Judaism of tomorrow. After my talk, a young, single woman in her twenties told me when she was finally ready to "date for real," meaning she wanted to only date people who were potential spouses, she talked to her friends and asked them to help set her up. When her friends asked her what she was looking for in a guy, she listed off a number of characteristics, including "Jewish."

Her friend looked at her aghast and chastised her, saying, "But that's so wrong. You don't even want to consider non-Jews? That's like a white person saying they don't want to date a black person. Don't you see how racist that is?!"

We need to start thinking of intermarriage as a plus-one, not a minus-one. Some may not like that it is happening, but it's a reality; so we need to embrace it and find ways to use it to make Judaism better. I fear that if we don't, and if we try to erect walls – like the first reaction to the social crash that Benay Lappe suggests – then we will inevitably push our young people into the opposite reaction to the crash, which is them walking away from doing Jewish altogether.

Israel and Israel-Diaspora Relations

Ironically, one of the most challenging and divisive factors leading to the need for an evolution in our Jewish OS has grown out of one of the greatest Jewish achievements of the last two thousand years: the creation of the modern State of Israel.

During the first week of October in 2000, when I worked for AIPAC, the American Israel Public Affairs Committee, I was sitting in my office in downtown San Francisco, overlooking Market Street, the main artery traveling through the financial district in the city. My colleagues and I heard shouting and we looked out the windows. Sure enough, there was some march going down the street. Now of course, this was San Francisco, so some march for some cause seemed to be going on every month. But this time they were waving giant Palestinian flags and holding posters with images of a child who'd recently been killed in the violence of the Second Intifada. So my boss and I decided to go down to have a closer look.

When we arrived, we saw that this was not just a "Pro-Palestinian rally," but a full-fledged anti-Israel rally. This was not the rallying cry of: "What do we want?! PEACE! When do we want it?! NOW!" They were shouting on bullhorns: "From the river to the sea, Palestine will be free!" They were not calling for coexistence, or even "separate but equal." They were burning Israeli flags – in the middle of San Francisco, people were burning flags with Jewish stars on them!

I wanted to jump in and rescue a burning blue and white flag, but my boss held me back. After the crowd moved on, I went in and grabbed the charred remnants of that flag and I brought it back to my office. I hung it up on my wall as a reminder of what I was fighting for...and against.

It was that moment, the height of the Second Intifada, when major cracks within the American Jewish community began to form. American Jews have always been concerned with Israeli decisions, policies, governments, actions, etc. – including the decision whether to even support the creation of a modern State of Israel. Since 1948, however, Israel has overwhelmingly been a unifying factor for American Jewry. Those who have had disagreements with Israel have been very few and usually on the fringes.

However, since the Second Intifada, more and more American Jews (mostly on the political left) have become frustrated with specific Israeli policies. Again, this is not a new phenomenon, but it has increased since 2000 to such a level that it can no longer be considered fringe. What began with Israel defending itself in a terrorist war led some Americans to voice their concerns with Israel's response. This trend coincided with the Israeli religious establishment introducing laws to curb the way non-Orthodox Judaism is practiced and recognized in Israel.[10]

---

10. I don't mean to suggest that American frustrations with Israel's treatment of non-Orthodoxy and Israel's treatment of the Palestinians grew chronologically in this way or out of each other. I only mean to suggest there was a coalescence of these two wedge issues around the same time – the beginning

What began to happen then and has only become more pronounced since, is that American Jews who disagree with Israel have begun to define their entire relationship with Israel by these areas of disagreement. This, in turn, has led more and more American Jews to publicly criticize Israel, pushing public criticism from the fringes into the mainstream; which has led, in turn, to more division within the American Jewish community itself: the political left versus right, secular versus religious, those who believe we should criticize publicly versus those who believe we should engage privately, etc. And that, in turn, has led to a cleavage in the relationship between American Jewry and Israel.

Yet, we are living in a truly historic moment. This is the first time ever in Jewish history that there is both a strong Jewish homeland and a strong Jewish Diaspora, primarily in America. This has never been the case before. We have had one or the other, but never both. Not until now.

With the establishment of the modern State of Israel, Jews have been free to help Judaism thrive without fear of antisemitism, pogroms, or Nazis. Jewish sovereignty has meant a state run by a Jewish calendar – with cities that shut down on Yom Kippur and shops that are mandated to close on Shabbat in some areas. It's meant Hebrew is the language of the sacred and the profane – from holy books to newspapers and from prayers to rock songs. It's meant a Jewish military to protect, defend, and rescue Jews all over the globe – from Entebbe to Ethiopia and from Yemen to Russia.

Simultaneously, the unprecedented freedoms afforded to

---

of the twenty-first century.

Jews in North America have allowed us to experiment openly with our Jewishness without fear of government-sponsored intervention. We have moved out of the synagogue and the home to light Hanukkah candles with Chabad in the busiest town squares in the country. We have democratized Jewish text study so it has moved out of the yeshiva and onto the internet with Sefaria, a website that provides free access and interconnectivity to every major Jewish text. We have revolutionized the rules around Jewish food, making kashrut about food justice and not just ritual slaughter. We have turned social action into a central part of Judaism so much so that *"tikkun olam"* is understood almost as widely as "oy vey!"

Because of this unique moment in time, these two centers of Jewish life are rubbing up against each other, and it's causing some friction. Unless we reimagine how Israel and the rest of the Jewish world engage with each other – especially when it comes to America, the strongest and largest Jewish community outside Israel – this friction will become worse and could lead to a "divorce" between them.

One important example has to do with defining "who is a Jew." In America, the vast majority of Jews are non-Orthodox. As we've already discussed, a majority of these Jews are marrying non-Jews. However, many of these non-Jews are indeed converting to Judaism before they marry. And it goes without saying that most of these conversions are being done by non-Orthodox rabbis. The problem is that Israel's Ministry of Religious Services will not recognize conversions done by non-Orthodox rabbis. That, of course, leads to a great deal of resentment by these American Jews.

To make matters even more complicated, Israel's Ministry of Absorption *does* recognize these converts as Jews, which means they are able to enjoy Israeli citizenship if they choose to immigrate to Israel. According to Israel's Law of Return, any Jew anywhere has the right to claim Israeli citizenship.[11] Once they immigrate, though, some Jews may not be permitted to engage in many Jewish ritual activities – like weddings and funerals – if they were not converted by an Orthodox rabbi. Micah Goodman, author of *The Wondering Jew*, said it quite poetically: "All Jews are welcome, but their preferred form of Judaism might not be."[12] Even those who were born to Jewish mothers and are seen as legally Jewish by the Chief Rabbinate will face challenges in Israel if they want to engage in a non-Orthodox Jewish ritual that needs state sanction, like a wedding.

This debate is not going away any time soon. In fact, it's only going to become more heated, especially since a landmark decision by Israel's Supreme Court on March 1, 2021 ruled that conversions done inside Israel by rabbis from the Reform and Masorti (Conservative) movements must be recognized as legitimate for purposes of Israeli citizenship. The Orthodox establishment in Israel immediately criticized the decision, teeing up the next phase of this ugly battle that surely will continue for many years to come.

There are other areas of tension as well. For instance, many Israelis feel that American Jews don't have a right to have a say in what happens in Israel since they don't live there, they don't pay taxes there, they don't serve in the military, etc.

---

11.   The text of the Law of Return can be viewed at https://www.knesset.gov.il/laws/special/eng/return.htm.

12.   Micah Goodman, *The Wondering Jew: Israel and the Search for Jewish Identity* (New Haven: Yale University Press, 2020), 15.

Yet many Americans would like to have a say in Israeli policies even beyond the religious ones. Israel's treatment of the Palestinians, for example, is an area that causes some American Jews great consternation. These Jews would like to have a say in Israeli policy because they feel that Israel is their homeland too. Some of these Jews also feel that American financial aid and perhaps even their own philanthropic support of Israel buys them a right to have a say. Just as they love America but lobby loudly to change its policies, they want to lobby loudly to change Israel's policies too. This mindset, by the way, is leading to major divisions among American Jews who don't share the same opinion on weighing-in on internal Israeli policies.

Since the turn of the twenty-first century, there have been constant attempts to politicize Israel, which since its founding has always been a bipartisan or non-partisan issue in American politics. On the one hand, liberal movements like The Women's March and Black Lives Matter have attempted to attach the Palestinian cause to their agendas,[13] which is causing severe cognitive dissonance amongst liberal Jews. They feel that to embrace their progressivism, they have to check their Zionism at the door.

On the other hand, conservative movements like the

---

13. See Farah Stockman, "Women's March Roiled by Accusations of Antisemitism," *New York Times*, December 23, 2018, https://www.nytimes.com/2018/12/23/us/womens-march-anti-semitism.html, and "Black Lives Matter, American Jews, and Antisemitism: Distinguishing Between the Organization(s), the Movement, and the Ubiquitous Phrase," Jewish Council for Public Affairs, July 16, 2020, https://www.jewishpublicaffairs.org/black-lives-matter-american-jews-and-antisemitism-distinguishing-between-the-organizations-the-movement-and-the-ubiquitous-phrase/.

Evangelical group Christians United For Israel have come out forcefully in favor of Israel. This is leading to a similar cognitive dissonance among conservative Jews, who are embracing their Zionism and checking their other issues at the door, like a woman's right to choose and LGBTQ rights.

While some believe that Israel's conservative politics have been making American Jews, who are overwhelmingly more liberal, pull away from Israel over the last two decades, I believe Rabbi Daniel Gordis gets it right when he makes the case in his book, *We Stand Divided: The Rift Between American Jews and Israel*, that Israeli and American democracies are fundamentally different animals and need to be viewed from very different perspectives. Gordis writes, "although most observers...believe that the fraught relationship is due to what Israel *does*, a closer look at the Jewish communities in Israel and the United States suggests that the real reason has to do with what Israel *is*."[14]

Regardless of why, the bottom line is that the polarization has become so extreme that for nearly two decades, many Jewish organizations in America simply refuse to touch the topic of Israel at all. They're too scared to even wade into the waters, worried that if they bring a speaker who leans too far left, their conservative donors will walk away; and if they bring a speaker that leans too far right, their liberal base will protest and leave.

One synagogue I was a member of was so worried about the issue they would not bring in any speaker on Israel, fearing it was too controversial. Yet they brought a speaker who

---

14. Daniel Gordis, *We Stand Divided: The Rift Between American Jews and Israel* (New York: Ecco, 2019), 8.

talked about why *brit milah* – the ancient and holy Jewish tradition of circumcising eight-day-old boys – was atrocious and should be outlawed!

The friction between Israel and American Jewry is more pronounced in younger generations. According to the Pew survey of Jewish Americans in 2020,

> Among Jews ages fifty and older, fifty-one percent say that caring about Israel is essential to what being Jewish means to them, and an additional thirty-seven percent say it is important but not essential; just ten percent say that caring about Israel is not important to them. By contrast, among Jewish adults under thirty, one-third say that caring about Israel is essential (thirty-five percent), and one-quarter (twenty-seven percent) say it's not important to what being Jewish means to them.[15]

Meanwhile, Israeli Jews seem to care about American Jews, but are also worried about where the relationship stands currently. According to another poll, ninety-five percent of Israelis feel that they have a moral obligation to the Jews of the Diaspora, but only fifty-seven percent believe the relationship is in a good place.[16]

The contemporary Zionist thought leaders Natan Sharansky and Gil Troy make this point poetically in their book

15. "Jewish Americans in 2020," Pew Research Center, Washington, D.C., May 2021, https://www.pewforum.org/2021/05/11/jewish-americans-in-2020/.

16. "New Survey: Israelis Morally Obligated to Diaspora Jews," March 7, 2019, https://jewishjournal.org/2019/03/07/new-survey-israelis-morally-obligated-to-diaspora-jews/.

Never Alone, writing, "True, we sometimes seem to be one people divided by one religion. And sometimes we seem to be one people divided by one state. But we remain one people."[17]

At the end of the day, barring a massive Jewish tragedy that brings us back together on a large scale, I believe if we don't alleviate this friction, then a future generation of American and Israeli Jews could simply just walk away from each other, which would be the real, long-lasting tragedy. So, a new Jewish Operating System must also involve a new paradigm on Israel-World Jewry relations reminding all of us that we are indeed one people.

Broadened Search for Meaning and Belonging

The fourth meta-trend contributing to a need for an evolution in the Jewish Operating System is the ability for people to find meaning and belonging outside their Jewish circles. This has existed on and off since the Hellenization of the Jews, but ever since the Enlightenment this reality has become more widespread. It has become even more pronounced since Jews have become more accepted in western, democratic societies.

Every year since 1988, thousands of people gather for a week-long festival in the vast, harsh, open desert of Black Rock City, Nevada called Burning Man. For many of the attendees, called Burners, this is the most spiritual and most connected they feel all year long. They often come home and try to recreate that feeling, but they can't quite make it happen back in the real world.

In 2007, a group of Jewish Burners associated with a

---

17. Natan Sharansky and Gil Troy, *Never Alone: Prison, Politics, and My People* (New York: Hachette Book Group, 2020), 428.

camp called Milk + Honey began hosting an open Shabbat service and dinner. Over the next ten years, the gathering grew and grew so that by 2019, over one thousand Burners celebrated Shabbat on the playa. According to one of the founding members of Milk + Honey, most of these folks never attend synagogue or celebrate Shabbat back home, but there is something about that environment that creates a deep sense of meaning and belonging for them. There is something about being back in the desert that provokes a spiritual urge and makes these participants want to connect to their roots.

I hear countless stories from people who find their sense of meaning and belonging in other non-religious settings as well. For some, it's a boot camp class or a Soul Cycle group, for others it's a book club or a mother's group. One place where Jews and others are finding their primary source of connection and belonging is in their political circles. Many Jews in Silicon Valley feel more comfortable among a group of people who share the same political views than a group with mixed political views. In fact, they no longer want to affiliate with Jewish groups that have participants with different political views from theirs.

When Donald Trump took office as president in 2017, one event after another popped onto the radar of the local Jewish community in Silicon Valley, prompting partisan outrage by Democrats. Whether it was Trump's executive order around the treatment of immigrants to the US, his comments about white supremacists, his rollback of environmental reforms, accusations of his treatment of women, and even acts of antisemitic violence that occurred "on his watch," it seemed that every month another event prompted the leadership of the local Jewish community to debate whether we needed to issue some sort of response based on a perceived violation of Jewish values.

It came to a head for the OFJCC when, in 2018, after the horrific shooting at the Tree of Life Synagogue outside of Pittsburgh, some of the JCC's leadership felt that Trump's attitude, comments and dog whistles had green-lighted antisemites to rise up and take the murderous action. This prompted the OFJCC Board of Directors to debate what kind of statement the organization should issue in the wake of the tragedy. Of course, everyone was on board with issuing a statement of support and sympathy for the Pittsburgh community, but there was disagreement around whether we should also condemn Trump's behavior in the same breath.

Ultimately, the organization chose to make a non-political statement, as we felt it was not our role, nor would such a statement impact the situation on the ground. Nevertheless, some members of the Jewish community trolled me personally on social media, claiming that Jewish communal leaders need to be moral voices and I was shirking my responsibility by not also specifically condemning Trump's actions.

Many rabbis across the country have been similarly shamed for what congregants (or even non-congregants) feel is them not taking a strong enough political stand. Others have chosen to speak from the pulpit or on social media about their political opinions, which has driven some to drop their membership to the synagogue and move elsewhere. This is leading to increased polarization among our congregations, so much so that it has led some to posit that we will soon have Democratic synagogues and Republican synagogues. Rabbi

Lord Jonathan Sacks said that, by doing this, "American Jewry is making a big, big, big mistake."[18]

These examples point to a trend of more and more Jews finding their sense of meaning and belonging in non-religious environments. Sarah Hurwitz, speechwriter for President Barack Obama and author of *Here All Along*, observes that while she came to see Judaism as a source for true meaning in her life after enrolling in an Introduction to Judaism class at the Washington, D.C., JCC, by contrast "Many search outside of established religious traditions, drawn to individuals who offer a variety of spiritual services, including healing experiences and practices that evoke intense highs."[19]

Theologians Angie Thurston and Casper ter Kuile of Sacred Design found that millennials are less religiously affiliated than ever before, yet they are "flocking to a host of new organizations that deepen community in ways that are powerful, surprising, and perhaps even religious."[20]

For Jewish life to stay relevant for this generation and beyond, we will have to look outside the walls of synagogues and traditional institutions when we design an updated Jewish Operating System.

---

18. Laura Adkins, "Rabbi Jonathan Sacks on Cancel Culture, Restoring Morality and Israel's Missed Opportunities," *Jewish Telegraphic Agency*, August 27, 2020, https://www.jta.org/2020/08/27/opinion/rabbi-jonathan-sacks.

19. Sarah Hurwitz, *Here All Along: Finding Meaning, Spirituality, and Deeper Connection to Life – in Judaism (After Finally Choosing to Look There)*, (New York: Random House, 2019), xxi.

20. Angie Thurston and Casper ter Kuil, "How We Gather," Sacred Design, published October 2019, https://sacred.design/wp-content/uploads/2019/10/How_We_Gather_Digital_4.11.17.pdf.

Evolution of Technology and Science

The final factor that is forcing us to rethink our Jewish Operating System are the blindingly fast changes in the worlds of science and technology. Judaism has always adapted to modernity. This is a central part of Judaism's ability to survive. We adapt while also holding on to our roots. We evolve while remaining true to our heritage. We find ways to hold both the old and the new in our hands at the same time.

I am reminded of a young man who moved to Silicon Valley from New York several years ago for a job. Unfortunately, he had an uncomfortable parting with his family back in New York because they were traditional, and when he told them he was gay, they didn't accept it at first. This was incredibly painful for him, but eventually he found a partner whom he fell in love with and who loved him back.

When it was time for him and his Hindu partner to find a community in the Bay Area, they wanted a place that would be open to accepting both of them but also provide deep, thoughtful, profound spiritual connection for them as well. They didn't find a synagogue that fit their needs, but they found the OFJCC and specifically a group that was studying Jewish texts here in an ongoing class. This class has a reputation for going deep thanks to the brilliance of the teachers, and it was just what someone like this young man, who had been raised in a traditional environment, needed.

When COVID hit, the classes had to move online and meet by Zoom. This was difficult, of course, as it's harder to make connections when you're not seeing each other in person. However, it gave this young man's mother back in New York the chance to join the classes by Zoom as well. So, she did.

And it opened her eyes to the loving relationship her son has with his partner and his willingness to hang on to his Jewish tradition.

The son's relationship with his mother has since been reignited, and it's an example of how something may not have happened but for the power of new technology.

There is precedent for adapting laws to keep up with science, and the laws around Shabbat are a good example. The rules surrounding the observance of Shabbat came from the days of the First Temple, and obviously life has changed since then. These laws became restrictive in the years since the Temple, and so the rabbis created "legal fictions," or work-arounds so they could honor the letter of the law, if not the spirit of the law.

One law, for example, says that you are not permitted to carry something outside the walls of your home. So the rabbis decided it was permissible to erect fake walls (an *eruv*) around the city which would allow them to carry items like a prayer book and *tallit* from their home to the synagogue.

Another law says you can't make fire on Shabbat. This law still stands to this day, but it has become more complicated with the invention of electricity. Now the prohibition includes creating an electrical circuit, but the rabbis found ways to adapt here, too. For example, if someone lives on a very high floor in a building and is unable to take the stairs, they can take a "Shabbat elevator" – one that stops automatically on every other floor so they don't have to push a button and create an electrical circuit.

Nevertheless, with the pace of change today, I fear that Judaism will not be able to keep up without major changes to its rituals, customs, and even laws. I will share a few examples here.

First of all, cloned meat is creating all sorts of challenges and opportunities within the laws of kashrut. A 2018 article in the *New York Times* described how scientists have figured out how to clone pigs, and it posited that bacon made from cloned pigs may indeed be kosher. Rabbi Gavriel Price of the Orthodox Union kosher certifying organization said, "I'd like to spend more time [studying the matter], because I think it's an important process to understand in a deep way, and there's no precedent for it really."[21]

Of course, the traditionalists will blanche at the prospect, believing that even if you put lipstick on a cloned pig, it's still a pig. Some may test the waters slowly, while I'm sure others will excitedly embrace this rabbinic ruling whole hog.

Second, self-driving cars are quickly becoming a reality. A headline in *Business Insider* back in 2016 predicted there would be ten million self-driving cars on the road by 2020.[22] While that clearly didn't happen, we are getting closer. What will it mean for getting around on Shabbat if you can ride in a self-driving car that's been pre-programmed to take you to your destination? We have ovens that are pre-programmed to go on at a certain hour, why couldn't cars do the same thing? Undoubtedly the traditionalists will have an issue with this

---

21. Nathaniel Popper, "Meat Labs Pursue a Once-Impossible Goal: Kosher Bacon," *New York Times*, September 30, 2018, https://www.nytimes.com/2018/09/30/technology/meat-labs-kosher-bacon.html.
22. "10 Million Self-Driving Cars Will Be on the Road by 2020," *Business Insider*, June 15, 2016, https://www.businessinsider.com/report-10-million-self-driving-cars-will-be-on-the-road-by-2020-2015-5-6.

work-around, but others will embrace the evolution of this Shabbat technology.

Third, virtual reality goggles are making it very realistic to be in a totally different time and place. Soon we'll be able to put on VR goggles and stand at the base of Mt. Sinai to be a part of the revelation of the Torah; we'll be able to experience a pogrom of Cossacks in Russia; we could witness firsthand the declaration of independence of the State of Israel in 1948; and we could watch Kristallnacht in Germany in 1938. What will it mean for creating a minyan, when VR goggles can put us in the room with nine others? Again, the rabbis who interpret the laws most traditionally will say no, but undoubtedly others will approve this new tool.

Fourth, what is going to happen when do-it-at-home DNA testing kits identify a "Jewish gene"? Already we can tell if we are ninety-eight percent Ashkenazi – as I am – from kits like those provided by 23andMe. According to the 23andMe website,

> DNA clearly shows connections among those who consider themselves to be Ashkenazi Jewish: two Ashkenazi Jewish people are very likely to be "genetic cousins," sharing long stretches of identical DNA. This reflects the fact that the Ashkenazi Jewish population expanded relatively recently from a small initial population.

How far away are we from digging even deeper into the "Jewish genome," and what will be the ramifications of such a discovery? How will genetic engineering be forever altered if indeed such a gene is identified? And what will it mean for

Jews who don't have the DNA to support their claims of Jewishness?

Finally, the outbreak of COVID19 in 2020 has led the Jewish community to find a plethora of new ways to connect through technology. In the first weeks of global lockdowns, even though many of us hosted virtual Passover Seders, the Chief Rabbinate in Israel was still prohibiting it.[23] But as the pandemic continued – along with social distancing – others in the Orthodox establishment in Israel began to innovate to incorporate virtual connectivity. By the time the High Holidays rolled around in the early fall of 2020, the Orthodox Union was offering resources to enjoy your "*chag* [holiday] at home."

Mainstream Jews haven't been as strict when it's come to virtual experiences and Jewish law. Most of us have been using the virtual space since the beginning of the pandemic lockdown to take care of religious business. As I mentioned earlier, when my family was forced to decide whether we wanted to continue my son Elie's bar mitzvah by doing it on Zoom or postponing it, we decided to move forward and do it virtually. It took a ton of time, patience, and creativity, but ultimately, we all loved what we pulled off.

One of the great benefits of using technology was having family and friends from thousands of miles away, who would never have been able to fly to an in-person bar mitzvah, participate. Similarly, when our rabbi gave her annual Yom Kippur sermon this year and mentioned that her parents were Zooming in, she had a huge smile on her face. I drew one

---

23. Daniel Villarreal, "Israel's Chief Rabbinate Says That Despite Coronavirus, Jews Cannot Hold Seder Over Zoom on Passover," *Newsweek*, April 1, 2020, https://www.newsweek.com/1495650.

major conclusion from these experiences: now that we can connect to our family from afar during rituals and life-cycle events, there will be no going back. The future will involve some hybrid of in-person and online experiences so we can make sure our aging grandparents are always able to join us.

Our ability to connect through social media or be present through virtual reality, our need to defer decision-making to artificial intelligence or find new ways to honor the Sabbath while traveling or eating differently, and the way we think, convene, pray, and experience life are fundamentally changing. What will these changes mean for doing and being Jewish when they reach a tipping point? What are the key challenges and opportunities we will face? Who will get to decide?

These are some of the questions determining the future of Jewish life. While I'm not sure I have the answers, I will attempt to offer some suggestions in the next chapter.

PART 3
HOW TO DO JEWISH?

4

Architecting a Jewish Future: Five Responses

In 2019, I took my daughter Talia, who was then fifteen, to her first AIPAC Policy Conference in Washington, D.C. It was the year when AIPAC was focusing on its relationships with the progressive community, reminding the community that it is a bipartisan organization. Over the course of the three days, a variety of speakers graced the stage, including Latinx leaders, African American leaders, and leaders from the Asian American community.

At one point during the plenary session, AIPAC was showing off its broad coalition of student activists on college campuses, and an African American student named Ellis Walton from Morehouse College mentioned how his Zionism was a part of his Christian beliefs. My daughter was stunned. She turned to me and said, "Wait. Aren't all these speakers Jewish?"

It never occurred to her that someone who looked very different from her would *not* be Jewish. Just the opposite, in fact. She assumed they were all Jewish and she wondered why a non-Jew would support Israel.

I was thrilled. I felt that we had succeeded in teaching a

new generation that Jews can be any color, can speak any language, can eat any food, and still be fully Jewish. Compare this to my generation – and definitely the generations before me – for whom our Ashkenormative view of the world still leads many of us to assume that Jews look a certain way, speak a certain way, eat a certain way, etc. No one is more attuned to this than my Jewish Filipino executive assistant, by the way. (Okay, so I have to do a little work teaching my kids why Christians and Muslims have a connection to Israel too. But let's leave that aside for now.)

Others have written and spoken much more eloquently than I on this topic. In fact, over the 2020 High Holidays, Rabbi Angela Buchdahl from Central Synagogue in New York gave a moving sermon called "We Are Family: Rethinking Race in the Jewish Community" that went viral overnight. I highly recommend watching it. (It is available on Youtube.)

I share the story of my daughter only to make the point that today, it is becoming more commonly accepted that Jews can be any race, come from any country, speak any language as their mother tongue, consider any food their traditional Jewish food, etc. We still have a long way to go on this, but thankfully organizations like Be'chol Lashon are working hard to ensure that Jews of Color have their voices heard.

Now that we know what the Jews of the future will look like, we have to ask what the future of Jewish life might look like.

At the Oshman Family JCC, our vision is, "To be the architects of the Jewish future." We are located in the heart of Silicon Valley, which is where innovators and entrepreneurs are actually changing the very future of the entire world. They are breaking barriers and pushing the limits in every single industry – from genetic testing to space travel – so why not in Jewish life too?

I believe the last century of American Jewish life was built by the Jews of the East Coast. The Federation system came out of Boston, the JCC system came out of New York, and the mega-synagogues in the tristate area defined American Jews rituals for the last century. Even the more cultural aspects of Jewish identity came from East Coast Jews: from the Borscht Belt to Broadway, Jewish performers defined Jewish humor and theater; New York publishing houses, magazines, and newspapers defined Jewish art and literature; and from Katz's Deli to Russ and Daughters, Jews of New York defined what it meant to eat Jewish food.

But if East Coast Jews defined what it meant to *be* Jewish for the last century, I believe the Jews of Northern California could define what it means to *do* Jewish for next hundred years. I make this assumption because the Jewish community here has four traits essential to take on this challenge.

First, the Jews here have the predisposition to "move fast and break things."[1] We are trailblazers out here. We are willing to pave new paths and push boundaries. It is in our nature not to accept the prescribed way, but to buck the status quo.

Second, we have the motivation to do Jewish differently here. Many Jews out west are yearning for new frameworks, fewer restrictions, and more mashups in their spirituality. For

---

1.   "Move fast and break things" was Facebook's internal motto for most of its early years until 2014, at which point it changed to "Move fast with stable infra." See Samantha Murphy, "Facebook Changes Its ‹Move Fast and Break Things› Motto," *Mashable*, April 30, 2014, https://mashable.com/2014/04/30/facebooks-new-mantra-move-fast-with-stability/.

example, we want to celebrate meaningful life-cycle events unrelated to where we pay membership dues, and we want to combine elements from various traditions in finding our spiritual paths. In fact, I think it goes both ways. A Christian friend who hears me talk about this topic quite often said to me, "We like to incorporate Buddhist and Hindu practices in our lives, like meditation and yoga. I think Judaism can do the same thing and become highly relevant for non-Jews too."

Third, we have one of the largest populations of Israeli expats in North America per capita. The Jewish Community Federation and Endowment Fund commissioned a "Portrait of Bay Area Jewish Life and Communities" in 2018 and found that 350,000 Jews live in the area. According to the Israeli consulate, more than ten percent of them are Israeli. With so many Israelis living here, we have a unique opportunity to mesh Israeli Judaism with American Judaism for a new hybrid Judaism. (If you haven't heard the term Israeli Judaism, check out Shmuel Rosner's book *#IsraeliJudaism: Portrait of a Cultural Revolution*.)

Finally, we have the resources to make it happen here. This is the wealthiest Jewish community in our people's history. According to a *Wealth-X* report, the Bay Area outperformed New York fourteen to one in creating new billionaires in 2019,[2] and according to *Forbes Magazine*, of the top ten richest Americans, five of them live in Silicon Valley – and of those, three are Jewish.[3]

---

2. "The Wealth-X Billionaire Census 2019," *Wealth-X*, May 9, 2019, https://www.wealthx.com/report/the-wealth-x-billionaire-census-2019/.

3. Edited by Kerry A. Dolan with Chase Peterson-Withorn and Jennifer Wang, "The Definitive Ranking Of The Wealthiest Americans In 2020," accessed January 17, 2021, https://www.forbes.com/forbes-400/#6ca04a6b7e2f.

Of course, I must state the obvious, which is that I can't predict the future. I don't know what Jewish life at the end of this millennium will look like. But if we aspire to have an impact, then we need to blaze ahead and break some glass. In that spirit, I will offer some thoughts on what updates to our Jewish Operating System we could put in place to respond to those aforementioned five drivers of change.

David or Goliath? Betting on the Underdogs and Little Guys

In the last forty years, the Shalom Hartman Institute has become "a leading center of Jewish thought and education, serving Israel and North America" (according to its website). Today, under the leadership of Rabbi Donniel Hartman, it has five independent but interrelated centers, including a robust center in North America run by Yehuda Kurtzer that was launched in 2010. Today, there is hardly a JCC, synagogue, or major Jewish agency that doesn't bring in Shalom Hartman Institute scholars to boost their own Jewish thought leadership.

But Hartman, as the Institute is called colloquially, was not always so well known. It began just like so many start-ups, as a small idea birthed from a visionary leader. In 1976, Rabbi David Hartman founded the Shalom Hartman Institute in Jerusalem to help build a more pluralistic and tolerant Israeli society. In the early days, it was comprised of just a team of research scholars in the study and teaching of classical Jewish sources and contemporary issues of Israeli society and Jewish life. As more and more philanthropists and Jewish institutional leaders paid attention to the Institute – and invested in it – the operation grew into the global influencer it is today.

We must acknowledge that the large, legacy institutions that currently drive most of the major decisions in the Jewish world cannot and will not be the only entities in the Jewish ecosystem determining the Jewish future. The Federations may have dictated where Jewish dollars were allocated for the last century, but that won't likely continue for the next century. Major synagogues may have had the monopoly on determining how and when each city celebrated its collective Jewish rituals, but that role now needs to be shared with other Jewish organizations in each locality.

I don't believe synagogues will go away, nor should they. They play a vital role in Jewish life and will continue to do so. But with the exception of the creative, boundary-pushing synagogues led by charismatic leaders unafraid to take risks and rabbis who are true thought leaders, most synagogues will not be the places that inspire the next generation of Jews to do Jewish. It's likely that distinction will go to the Jewish start-ups carving a new path.

As for the larger institutions like JCCs, they need to make themselves a platform where the start-ups can experiment. They need to be amplifiers of the great stuff the little guys are doing. Instead of being content creators, JCCs and other large Jewish institutions need to be content providers, just like Lyft and Uber are massive taxi-cab companies that do not own a single taxi, and VRBO and AirBnB are the largest hotel companies in the world but they don't own a single hotel. That is the Jewish ecosystem of the future. The days of "vertical integration" within a singular Jewish institution are over.

In 2006, Rabbi Niles Goldstein published a wonderful book called *Gonzo Judaism: A Bold Path for Renewing an Ancient Faith* in which he made a similar argument regarding the start-ups in the Jewish world and offered a very comprehensive list of them at the time. Some are still going strong to this day, but others on the list have sadly pulled up tent stakes and moved on. Despite the challenges they face in surviving or succeeding, I'm going to share a few contemporary examples here from the new Jewish ecosystem (even if some of these will be forced to pull up their own tent stakes in the next twenty years).

UpStart is an organization that "partners with the Jewish community's boldest leaders to expand the picture of how Jews find meaning and how we come together." Since its inception in 2008 and the subsequent merging with Bikkurim, Joshua Venture Group, and PresenTense in the US, UpStart has supported over 1,450 exciting, innovative, and fresh new initiatives in the Jewish world. That's over one hundred new Jewish start-ups per year for the last twelve years – and those are only the ones who were accepted into UpStart's selective accelerator programs! That's a lot of interest and excitement from entrepreneurial Jews who are not receiving what they need from the old establishment. We need to listen to them.

Slingshot is another exciting organization doing work in this section of the Jewish institutional ecosystem. Its "Theory of Change" states, "The younger generation is not finding a meaningful place in Jewish life. This is happening because the Jewish community isn't doing enough to envision new models of Jewish life and to engage the next generation in shaping the Jewish future."

For the first thirteen years of its existence, Slingshot published an annual guide of the most exciting new organizations working in the Jewish world. In 2018, "after featuring more than three hundred organizations that have transformed

Jewish life for the better," they pivoted to guiding future philanthropists. And dare I say, these will be the funders of the Jewish future.

Of the more than 1,450 UpStarters and three hundred Slingshotters, I would like to highlight just a small handful of inspiring new organizations here, to make my point that the future is bright if we bet on the trailblazers and outsiders.

At the Well is an organization founded by Sarah Waxman whose mission is "to connect women around the world through transformative practices inspired by ancient Jewish Wisdom." They use written material rooted in ancient texts to inspire the creation and sustaining of "Well Circles," which are groups of six to twelve women who meet monthly to share stories and spiritual experiences. The circles are independently run, self-led and self-sustaining – a true grassroots movement. At the Well also runs retreats and workshops and facilitates other opportunities at women-centric events.

One Table was founded by Aliza Klein to "make Shabbat dinner accessible to tens of thousands of people who otherwise would be absent from Jewish community." The way they accomplish their goal is by providing Shabbat dinner hosts with the resources to do the Shabbat rituals, and they provide elements of the meal by subsidizing the costs. They offer literature, guides, meditations, and they even pivoted during COVID to create a "Shabbat Alone, Together" resource. One Table truly embodies the quote from Ahad Ha'am that "More than the Jewish People have kept Shabbat, Shabbat has kept the Jewish People."

Moishe House was founded in 2006 by David Cygielman to help Jewish young adults who "wanted to more actively engage in the Jewish community and were too old for Jewish life on campus and too young for the traditional young adult and family programming being offered." They created a concept of having a group of young Jews live together in a house where they'd host Jewish programs for their friends and community. Now, there are Moishe Houses in over twenty-seven countries, and they reach more than sixty thousand young adults around the world every year.

Wilderness Torah was founded by Zelig Golden "to awaken and celebrate the earth-based traditions of Judaism to nourish the connections between self, community, earth and Spirit." They offer a variety of programs that celebrate the environment and the outdoors from holiday celebrations for the High Holidays, Sukkot, and Passover, to Jewish study opportunities, to a b'nai mitzvah alternative called B'naiture, and a scouting initiative called Shomrim.

BINA: The Jewish Movement for Social Change was founded in 1996 after the assassination of Yitzhak Rabin because the founders believed they needed to create a solution to Israel's "breakdown in public trust and unity." BINA, "an Israeli-born movement at the intersection of Jewish education and social activism," is one of Israel's "secular yeshivas" that operate based on three principles: *limud* (study), *maaseh* (social action) and *kehillah* (community). They offer a space for those interested in deep learning but without the religious trappings that secular Israelis find challenging. BINA began in Israel but now has operations in several countries, including the US, where they partner with the OFJCC.

Honeymoon Israel was founded in 2014 by Avi Rubel and Mike Wise, who saw the data that showed many young Jews today are intermarrying and then dissociating with Judaism. They asked, "How do we better welcome young couples with diverse backgrounds to Jewish life so that we meet them were they are, rather than where the community might want them to be?" They created Honeymoon Israel to send intermarried couples from the same city to Israel to connect to Judaism and to each other so that when they return from their trip, they have a new community of Jewish friends and a deeper connection to Jewish life.

OpenDor Media was launched in 2009 with a mission to educate and entertain millions of people around the world by producing and distributing Jewish and Israel content through digital media. They claim to "drive outsized impact by using today's most popular and far-reaching digital platforms," including all the social media and internet-based products available today. They are especially plugged in to young people, millennials and Gen Zers, and they also work with educators around the globe to ensure their content is being used to help users "lead more informed and connected Jewish lives."

I need to add one other organization to this list, though it looks nothing like the others. Indeed, in some ways it is exactly the opposite of the others, as it is old-school, prayer-based, synagogue-centric, and very traditional. And yet, it is remarkably effective. It's **Chabad**.

According to their website, "Chabad-Lubavitch is a philosophy, a movement, and an organization. It is considered to be the most dynamic force in Jewish life today." Chabad is a branch of Chasidism that was founded 250 years ago, but expanded globally under the guidance of the Lubavitcher Rebbe, Rabbi Menachem Mendel Schneerson, in the late twentieth century. Today, Chabad has over five thousand full-time emissary families all over the globe, and at least part of their secret sauce is that once their emissaries embed themselves into communities, they don't leave. Unlike most other Jewish outreach groups that employ community organizers who might work somewhere for a few years and then move on to their next job, Chabad emissaries stay for life so their relationships become deep and authentic. Chabad has actually created a model that is worth studying and replicating by non-religious Jews for its incredible impact and effectiveness.

Chabad notwithstanding, the combination of organizations like UpStart and Slingshot, and the chutzpah and vision of leaders like Sarah Waxman, Aliza Klein, and David Cygielman, the Jewish community is creating a new ecosystem that will shape the future of Jewish life. These are the pioneers and newcomers to whom we must pay attention. Let's not forget that Judaism itself was the start-up not so long ago. Okay, so maybe it was more than three thousand years ago, but still, the Jewish People are definitely still the visionaries and outsiders when compared to the rest of the world.

Funny, You Don't Look Jewish: Embracing Radical Inclusivity[4]

In the summer of 1996, I was working for the JCCs in Los Angeles in the teen department, which meant I was responsible for helping to lead the JCC Maccabi Games delegation to New Jersey.

The JCC Maccabi Games are an annual sporting event for Jewish teenagers that take place in one to five different cities,

---

4.   "Funny, You Don't Look Jewish" is a commonly used title for books and articles dealing with the issue of Jewish ethnography.

depending on how many communities are able to host each summer. They attract an average of three thousand teens from across North America each year, and it's a wonderful bonding experience centered on Jewish values and Israeli culture for kids who care about playing sports at a serious level. In fact, it can get pretty competitive, especially in the final stages, i.e., the semifinals and finals.

The Los Angeles team had a strong reputation for putting together dominating teams on the basketball court. LA had hosted the games the year before, so we were expected to put together another winning team for the 1996 games.

We began receiving applications from kids and hosting tryouts to choose the best players. One basketball player in particular was head and shoulders above all the others – figuratively and literally. He was well over six feet tall, and his skill on the court was phenomenal. The coaches were giddy with excitement to have him join the team. But once they examined his application more closely, a problem arose.

The one non-negotiable rule for the JCC Maccabi Games is that the kids must be Jewish. Defining what that meant at the time was not very difficult for the Games committee. For them, it was simple: as long as the kid had a Jewish mother, he or she was Jewish. And in the case of our basketball player, they discovered his father was the Jewish parent, not his mother.

Well, you can imagine the efforts that went into trying to make sure this kid could play for the team. But at the time, there was no changing the rule – the athletes had to have a Jewish mother. So, sadly, this young man wasn't permitted to play for the team.

In the end, the LA basketball team did go on to win the gold medal at the New Jersey games that summer. And years later, the rule changed so that the athletes who want to play in the JCC Maccabi Games had to have a Jewish parent, but it could be their mother or father.

In his book *American Post-Judaism: Identity and Renewal in a Postethnic Society*, Professor Shaul Magid makes the following claim:

> Jews in America today do not *need* Judaism in order to identify as "Jewish," and they do not *need* to identify as "Jewish" or to identify with a Jewish collective (nor do they need to convert to some other religion) in order to live fully integrated lives in twenty-first-century America. Yet increasingly many Jews in America *want* to identify as Jews – even many who are married to non-Jews or who have one non-Jewish parent – and they *want* Judaism in some form to serve that identity. But they want it on *their* terms in part because of the *myth* of tradition no longer operates for them as authoritative. Moreover, being *ethnically* Jewish (Jewishness *sans* religion) is no longer sufficient when a growing minority – and soon, the majority – of American Jews are multiethnic. For many of them, being Jewish is one part of a more complex narrative of identity.[5]

For Jewish Peoplehood to remain relevant for the next millennium, we must embrace radical inclusivity. But what exactly does that mean? Should we have no boundaries and barriers?

---

5. Shaul Magid, *American Post-Judaism: Identity and Renewal in a Postethnic Society* (Bloomington: Indiana University Press, 2013), 11.

Should anyone who celebrates Shabbat be included in the family? Should there be some basic litmus tests around ancestry? With DNA home testing kits readily available, this shouldn't be too hard, but just because we can, does that mean we should?

These are difficult questions, and I'm not sure I can answer them all. But I believe we must ask them, and debate them, and begin to answer them. So here, I will offer my incomplete answers to many of them.

First, we must celebrate the fact that Jews can be found on every continent, speaking every language and representing every ethnicity. Our institutions may not always make them feel welcome initially – and shame on us for that – but I believe this is changing. Surely the transformation is coming too slowly, but groups like Jews of Color Initiative are working every day to ensure our Jewish insititutions are representative of the full spectrum of Jewish identities, while groups like Be'chol Lashon are raising awareness of our racial and cultural diversity for the whole community. So, I am optimistic that this part of the radical inclusivity equation will change for the better within a generation.

Second, the ethos of radical inclusivity must treat families where one parent is Jewish and the other is not as full members of our community. For nearly all non-Orthodox Jews today, if someone had one Jewish parent – even if it is the father – they are considered Jewish. This goes against the requirement of matrilineal descent, so it is not and will not be accepted by Orthodox Jews. However, even Israel utilized the same logic of the Nuremberg Laws as the basis of the state's initial legal definition of a Jew, which says if you have one Jewish grandparent, on either side, you're Jewish.

As I said, the one Jewish parent definition is being accepted by the majority of American Jews today. However, where we find some sticking points is when synagogues and rabbis delve into how that family practices their Judaism. Someone in our community in Silicon Valley recently related a story to me about the challenge he had when trying to do a Jewish baby naming ceremony for his daughter. He approached several Reform synagogues and rabbis and none of them doubted the Jewishness of his daughter – even though he was the Jewish member of the couple and his wife was not – but where he ran into trouble was when they asked how the family would practice their Judaism.

This father told the rabbis that he and his wife were going to raise their daughter with both Judaism and Christianity in their home. In each case, the rabbi chose not to do the baby naming. When this father asked why, at least one rabbi replied, "Because we don't want her bringing Jesus into the preschool, as that could influence the other kids." Ultimately, the father had one of the local JCC rabbis do the baby naming, and after raising his daughter with both religions for fifteen years, last year she asked to have a bat mitzvah. Better late than never, he said.

This is challenging, of course, because we need to ask where we draw the line. How far is indeed too far? Are there any practices or beliefs that are out of bounds? How about Jews for Jesus? Their tag line is "100% Jewish. 100% Christian." They claim they are a place for Jews who believe Jesus was the Jewish Messiah. But isn't that an internal contradiction? Can someone be a vegetarian if they eat meat? Or, keeping this Jewish, can someone consider themselves truly kosher if they eat non-kosher meat?

I'm reminded of the time one of my colleagues at AIPAC,

Jonathan Kessler, was working with pro-Israel students on a college campus in Washington State and he took one to lunch. He asked the student if he ate kosher, and the student said yes. But then when they ordered their sandwiches, the student ordered a ham and cheese sandwich. Jonathan looked at him curiously and said, "I thought you said you eat kosher?..." The student replied, "I do. I eat kosher and non-kosher. I eat everything!"

But I digress. My point is that I do believe there are some beliefs and actions that are out of bounds for being considered Jewish. You can celebrate Christmas because you have a Christian parent, but that is not Jewish. It's not a Jewish custom. It's not a Jewish holiday. And it is not based in Jewish values – it celebrates the birth of Jesus. However, just because you celebrate it, that doesn't make you a non-Jew. You may also celebrate Hanukkah because your other parent is Jewish – and that *is* a Jewish holiday based on Jewish customs and traditions.

Celebrating Christmas and Hanukkah does not make you off-limits to the Jewish People, either. You should still be welcomed and embraced, though I acknowledge it's complicated. Fortunately, there are organizations out there like 18Doors that are helping navigate these uncharted waters. 18Doors's mission is to "[empower] people in interfaith relationships – individuals, couples, families and their children – to engage in Jewish life and make Jewish choices, and [encourage] Jewish communities to welcome them."

Finally, what about the non-Jews who live a Jewish life? Should we include them too? How should we include them? What should we call them? Are they part of the Jewish People, or are they asterisked like the 2020 Major League Baseball season that only played sixty games?

First of all, I think it's important to ask *them* how they want to be recognized. In my experience, many of the non-Jews who live a Jewish life but have not converted to Judaism don't consider themselves Jewish; however, they do want the Jewish community to accept them and embrace them as part of the community. They are often married to Jews and raising their kids Jewish or at least partially Jewish, so they feel strongly that they ought to be appreciated for that. And I agree with them. Let's give them the big bear hug they deserve and make them feel welcomed into our Jewish family.

My last comment on this topic for now is the following: throughout this section, I've continued to say, "The Jewish People must accept..." as if there were some Council of Elders who are the arbiters of these decisions. I know that's not the case for the non-Orthodox community, though FDR purportedly quipped when having challenges working with the Jewish community during the Holocaust, "Why can't the Jews just have a pope that I could work with?" But I suppose I have in mind the large establishments like synagogues and the movements that support them, i.e., the Reform movement as represented by the URJ. And yes, I understand the internal contradiction here, that on the one hand I'm saying these large establishment institutions will become less important in the future and on the other hand, these institutions are the arbiters of these decisions. However, I suppose the point is: for these large institutions to *not* become irrelevant, they ought to embrace these suggestions. And if they don't, they might just march off into obsolescence.

I will end this section with the joke about the Jewish

mother who goes to watch her son in the school marching band, and when she returns her friend asks, "Nu? How was it?" And the mother replies, "Well, my son was excellent. But all the other kids were out of step."

Let's help the large establishment organizations help themselves, lest they find themselves out of step with the rest of the band.

Z3: Evolving a Zionist Ideology for the Twenty-First Century

During my fourteen years at AIPAC, I worked tirelessly to advance the US-Israel relationship. I devoted the majority of my waking hours to this cause – and more than a few sleepless nights as well. I spoke to countless audiences about the need for American Jews to support the US-Israel relationship, regardless of who was in power and what policies were being promoted. I lobbied congressmembers hundreds of times about the vital necessity of supporting our number one ally in the world, despite their concerns over some of the most controversial issues, such as the occupation, settlements, targeted assassinations, the security barrier, unilateral disengagements, checkpoints, and more.

But what I observed over this decade and a half was that the rift between American Jewry and Israel was only widening. It was getting worse, not better. I saw many American Jews wagging their fingers at Israel because they didn't approve of Israel's treatment of the Palestinians or the Israeli Chief Rabbinate's positions regarding non-Orthodox Jews. Meanwhile, many Jews in Israel started shrugging their shoulders at American Jews, saying Diaspora Jewry wouldn't exist in a generation due to assimilation and antisemitism. Some Israeli leaders were calling intermarriage the "next Holocaust,"[6] and many Israelis couldn't understand what American Jewry had to offer to the future of Jewish life.

Ultimately, I saw us talking past each other and felt it was long overdue for us to rise above our differences, time to elevate our relationship. I believed then, as I do now, that we must transcend what divides us and focus on what unites us. I vowed to do something to make it stop. So, when I became CEO of the OFJCC in the summer of 2013, I realized that with this new platform I had the opportunity to do something about this rift. I had the chance to create something that could help us work through our disagreements, something that could create a new paradigm for Israel-Diaspora relations.

In the fall of 2015, with the partnership of *Haaretz* newspaper, we hosted the first Zionism 3.0 Conference at the OFJCC. It was a conference where we set out to bring together the left and the right, the Orthodox and the secular, the Israelis and the Americans, the settlers and the Tel Avivniks. We wanted to bring speakers from the left that ZOA would never bring to its conference, like Peter Beinart, and speakers on the right that J Street would never bring, like Israeli Deputy Foreign Minister Tzipi Hotovely. And it worked. We sold out the conference with over eight hundred attendees and have gone on to host even more successful conferences since then.

This is an exciting and effective example of how we can

---

6. "Israel's New Education Minister Calls Intermarriage in US a Second Holocaust," *Jewish Telegraphic Agency*, July 9, 2019, https://www.jta.org/quick-reads/israels-new-education-minister-calls-intermarriage-in-u-s-like-a-second-holocaust.

bridge the divide between world Jewry and Israel. But more efforts like this are needed.

We call this effort Zionism 3.0. Why Zionism 3.0? Because we may be at the third iteration of Zionist ideology.[7] I contend that Zionism 1.0 was the pre-1948 Zionism of theory, of the pioneers, of Zionist thinkers and statesmen including Theodor Herzl, Ahad Ha'am, and Rabbi Abraham Isaac Kook. It was the Zionism of creating a sovereign Jewish state where Jews could be safe and could live a Jewish life without fear of pogroms or Nazis.

Then in 1948, Zionism evolved to its next phase, the Zionism of reality, of the builders like Prime Ministers David Ben-Gurion, Menachem Begin, Golda Meir, and Yitzhak Rabin. Israel's existence was threatened by its neighbors every decade for the first sixty years of its life, and a vital piece of its survival was Diaspora support. Zionism 2.0 was the Zionism defined by the "rich American uncle" – the notion that those of us in the Diaspora who didn't make aliyah must support those who had. It was the Zionism of Diaspora negation; the thinking that the Jewish future lies only in Israel, and those of us living in the Diaspora were somehow lesser Jews.

But now Israel is strong. And American Jewry is also strong. We have different characteristics, to be sure, but we are both flourishing. We now depend on each other in new ways, and we can enrich each other in new ways! So, the model must evolve to Zionism 3.0, the next phase of Zionist ideology.

These two major centers of Jewish life are blossoming, and we must create a new paradigm for how we engage with

---

7.   Some of this section is reprinted from an article I wrote in November 2020 that can be found on Jweekly.com

each other – a way that takes us beyond our political and re-ligious differences. We must find a way to work together, to share what's special, and to fix what frustrates us about the other, *together*, through a consultative relationship, not an old, paternalistic, finger-wagging relationship.

We must recognize that Jews in both places *add* to the other – not just for security, but with each other's spiritual and cultural contributions as well. That's why we should *not* let political frameworks dictate the nature of our relationship. We should use our shared sense of Peoplehood and let our common destiny frame our relationship.

I am under no delusions that we are going to iron out all our differences. We will need to wait for the Messiah for that to happen – and even then, who knows? We've seen that argu-ment play out before!

But the Jewish People have been divided since the very beginning. Joseph and his brothers didn't get along so well, of course. And then there were the Sadducees and Pharisees who *really* disagreed with each other. The famous sages Hillel and Shammai couldn't even agree on how to light Hanukkah candles! Even during our darkest hour, during the Shoah, Jew-ish partisan fighters disagreed with the Jewish councils in the ghetto over how best to save Jewish lives; yet in the end, both groups came together in feeling like they could have done more. When the modern State of Israel was being reborn, the Irgun and the Haganah fought for the liberation of Israel *and* battled with each other!

So, we have never agreed. And we never will. But that's not the point. Throughout our history, we have remained sib-lings. Brothers and sisters. And that's the paradigm I want to propose: Brotherhood. Sisterhood. We are siblings.

Siblinghood is even stronger than marriage. You can't divorce your brother. Yes, you can fight with each other. As we've seen, you can go to war with each other. But siblings are still siblings 'til the end.

Just as we rescued Jews from the former Soviet Union without asking about their politics or the level of their religious observance – we just embraced them and called them brothers and sisters – so too must we embrace each other today, Israeli Jews and Diaspora Jews, beyond our political or religious differences.

We are family. We share a legacy and a destiny, and we must find a new way to engage with each other. The Z3 Project attempts to do exactly that by embracing three central principles:

1. Unity, not uniformity: we aim to honor our differences while working for the oneness of the Jewish People.

2. Engaging as equal partners: we bring together Israelis and Diaspora Jews to build our common future.

3. Diversity of voices: we convene Zionists of differing backgrounds and perspectives across the political and religious spectrums.

For the last six years, the OFJCC has hosted a full-day conference that's attracted over a thousand people at a time to engage in this conversation. In 2020, due to COVID, the experience was available to people all over the world by moving to a fully virtual experience over the week of Hanukkah. This innovative online experiment was so much more than just a web conference. Thanks to the partnership of JCC Association of North America and JCC Global, more than thirty JCCs brought Z3 to their own communities, and what we learned is that there is a real hunger for these conversations around the world.

For Jewish Peoplehood to remain meaningful, relevant, and joyous in the twenty-first century, we need to reimagine Diaspora-Israel relations. We need to find a new way to engage with each other. Natan Sharanksy and Gil Troy make this plea in their book *Never Alone* when recounting the rift between Diaspora Jewry and Israel over the struggle to incorporate new Ethiopian Jewish immigrants into Israeli society. They highlight the need for a third era in Zionist ideology as they look back and recollect on that moment, remembering, "The road to the third stage of mutual dependence, when we realize that we needed one another as equal partners, remained to be paved."[8]

It's time to pave that road, the third road, that will lead the Jewish People into the twenty-first century together as one.

Making Our Own Shabbos: Reinventing Jewish Rituals and Holidays

I shared in the last chapter the story of how the Milk + Honey camp at Burning Man established a tradition of making a Shabbat meal on Friday night that attracts over one thousand people. What I didn't share is that one of the founders of the Milk + Honey camp used to work at the OFJCC. In addition to being a die-hard Burner, this individual was always looking for the most exciting, engaging, and creative ways to innovate Jewish life. If you put those two traits together, then you can

---

8. Natan Sharansky and Gil Troy, *Never Alone: Prison, Politics, and My People* (New York: Hachette Book Group, 2020), 333.

understand how we created a new ritual around the holiday of Lag b'Omer.

Lag b'Omer is a lesser-known holiday that occurs on the thirty-third day of the Omer, which is the forty-nine-day period between Passover and Shavuot when traditional Jews mourn the death of tens of thousands of disciples of Rabbi Akiva who died in a plague during that time. There is no single, definitive reason why we celebrate Lag b'Omer, which is a one-day break from the mourning period, but it is often associated with Simeon Bar Yochai, a great Jewish mystic who's been credited with writing the Zohar, the key work of Kabbalah. Lag b'Omer represents a break from the period of semi-mourning during the Omer and is often celebrated with bonfires – especially in Israel, where even the non-religious Jews enjoy a springtime beach party around a giant bonfire.

Most American Jews have no idea about Lag b'Omer, but at the OFJCC, we thought it was time to resurrect the holiday and make it relevant for our community. Since we identified a whole gaggle of Jewish Burners in the Bay Area, we decided to combine Lag b'Omer and Burning Man to create a new festival: Burning Mensch.

We hosted a giant Burning Mensch festival in our open parking lot complete with bonfires, fire-eaters, fire walkers, and fire art. While the sun was up, the festivities were quite family friendly, but when the sun went down, it became an adults-only party, and the booze came out. The community had a great time: they loved having a little taste of Burning Man back home for one night only; they loved coming together with folks they hadn't seen for the nearly nine months since the playa; and they loved that we invented a new Jewish ritual to accompany a traditional Jewish holiday.

This is just one example of how we must become creative with Jewish rituals and holidays if we expect our people to find meaning, relevance and joy in them. But it's not just up to the JCCs and other Jewish institutions. We need to empower all Jews to innovate and experiment so doing Jewish works for them.

Every spring, millions of Jews around the world host a Passover Seder. However, no two Seders will ever be identical. Some will lean toward treating the Haggadah like a book that's meant to be read from cover to cover, while others will pick and choose which pages they want to read or skip. Still others will piece together their own Haggadah from a collection of other Haggadot, articles, drawings, quotes, etc. And yet others won't even use a Haggadah at all, choosing a more performance-based method for telling the Exodus story.

During the COVID lockdown of 2020, REBOOT created an online Passover Seder experience called "Saturday Night Seder" that raised over $3 million for charity. The participants were actors and singers who performed, read, laughed, and otherwise created a new Seder experience for anyone who wanted to log in. This could become a new annual tradition going forward.

We've also seen how the Passover Seder, which is a potent symbol of freedom and liberation, has come to stand for a declaration of liberation from some other form of oppression over the years. At one time, we called for the release of Soviet Jews around our Seder tables. At other times, we called for women's liberation. Later, we used the Seder to call for LGBTQ rights, racial justice, and environmental justice. Still later, I heard of Seders being focused on calling for liberation from the tyranny of gun violence. In 2020, the Seder became a symbol for freedom from our captivity born of COVID lock-downs.

In each of these iterations, we've made the Passover Seder relevant for modern times. When you combine that with the fact that they are very family friendly and child-centric, Passover Seders are the epitome of a meaningful, relevant, and joyous Jewish holiday. It's no wonder they are the most celebrated Jewish practice out of all Jewish traditions. A 2014 Pew survey found that seventy percent of American Jews participated in a Passover Seder. Compare that to the next most widely practiced tradition, which is fasting for Yom Kippur – done by fifty-three percent of Jews. (Only twenty-three percent of American Jews light Shabbat candles, by the way.)[9]

I believe the ability to innovate and have fun with a Seder is a major reason why so many people participate in it and why the ritual has stayed alive for so many generations. That's exactly the model we need to embrace for all Jewish rituals and holidays.

The challenge is that many American Jews believe there is a "correct" or "authentic" way to engage in Jewish rituals and if they do it any other way, they'll feel like it doesn't count. The reality, however, is that we've been innovating rituals from the very beginning.

According to Dan Libenson from Judaism Unbound, we've been "borrowing" our traditions from others for a long time. He spoke specifically of the Hanukkah dreidel and pointed me

---

9. "Attending a Seder Is Common Practice for American Jews," Pew Research Center, Washington, D.C., April 2014, https://www.pewresearch.org/fact-tank/2014/04/14/attending-a-seder-is-common-practice-for-american-jews/

to an article in the *Forward* that attributes the *dreidel* to an old Irish gambling game:

> Although its exact origins are lost to history, a top that would later evolve into the dreidel was brought from Ireland (or perhaps England) to Germany during the late Roman period. Men would gamble with a top known as a "teetotum" in bars and inns. Originally the letters on the teetotum corresponded to the first letters of the Latin words for "nothing," "half," "everything," and "put in."[10]

So, there is a rich tradition in Judaism of reinventing rituals, even if we don't realize it. We ought to be open-minded about what else can be reinvented. For example, how can we make the bar or bat mitzvah more meaningful and relevant? Many kids today feel that laboring through years of Hebrew school for a coming-of-age ceremony and big party when they turn thirteen is worth it; but still many more would rather find a different path to arrive at that same milestone.

Under the leadership of Joy Levitt, the Marlene Meyerson JCC of Manhattan realized this, so they launched the Jewish Journeys Project, which is "an initiative designed to revolutionize Jewish education." Their B-Mitzvah Journey allows kids to choose a focus of their interest. Kids can choose between JBrick: Building Israel in LEGOS; Jewish History in Minecraft; Dungeons and Dreidels: Tall Tales of the Torah; or Jewish Arts

---

10. Jordan Kutzik, "Our Favorite Hanukkah Toy Was Actually a Non-Jewish Irish Gambling Game," *Forward*, December 9, 2015, https://forward.com/culture/326379/the-true-history-of-the-dreidel/.

Studio: The Jewish Art of Papercutting. I know that if I had had those options as a seventh grader, I would have enjoyed my pre-bar mitzvah education a whole lot more.

At the OFJCC, we offer a "Raise the Bar" b'nai mitzvah program for the children of Israelis who are not interested in a traditional synagogue bar or bat mitzvah experience. Kids who speak Hebrew can go through an immersive program that incorporates cultural experiences, traditional learning, social action projects, and communal gatherings with a culminating ceremony at the end that is not religious.

The bar mitzvah itself is a life-cycle event that's been iterated over the years. The term was first used in the fourteenth century as a moment when a young Jewish man was old enough to wear tefillin, but centuries later a ceremony and party was attached to marking the moment. Then, in 1922, the daughter of Rabbi Mordecai Kaplan became the first girl to have a bat mitzvah.[11]

As we move into the future, we should prepare more Jews to be able to engage in DIY (do it yourself) Judaism. As synagogues and institutions fail to speak to mainstream Jews, more of the regular Jews will still want to do Jewish, but they'll want to do it their own way. According to Barry Finestone from the Jim Joseph Foundation in a conversation we had, the answer is to double down on Jewish literacy so we can make Jews feel like they know enough to do their own thing. I'm inclined to agree.

Days United is a great example of a new initiative that helps families do DIY Judaism by providing a holiday-in-a-box

---

11. Rabbi John L. Rosove, "History of the Bar/Bat Mitzvah," *Reform Judaism*, September 8, 2014, https://reformjudaism.org/history-barbat-mitzvah.

for at least eight of the major annual holidays. (They also do holiday boxes for Indian and Chinese holidays.) They provide fun, creative ritual objects in a beautiful package with how-to links online.

There is something else we'll need to accept in this brave new world of reinventing Jewish holidays: *when* we celebrate them. For some, the date is sacrosanct: on Passover, we host a Seder; on Yom Kippur, we fast; on Purim, we read the megillah, etc. You don't engage in the ritual unless it's on the actual day. However, more and more young Jews and young families are picking convenient times to celebrate the holidays. I know examples of young adults who want to be with their family or friends to do a Passover Seder but don't feel that they can take off work to travel and prepare, so they set it up for the weekend closest to Passover.

Is this something we have to accept? Or should we push back on it? Should we insist that the holidays are celebrated on the days when the Hebrew calendar says we should, or can we be flexible? Dan Libenson reminds me that some American holidays rotate every year based on the day of the week, and he asks, "Mother's Day and Father's Day, for example, are always on a Sunday, so why can't we do the same with Jewish holidays?"

Something else to ask ourselves is what we should throw out. What are the parts of the rituals and holidays we should retire, and which are the sacred cows that should never go away? Or are there no sacred cows?

I'm not sure I have a good answer to these questions, but I'm not sure I need to. I think the point is that to make Jewish life meaningful, relevant, and joyous for the next hundred years, we need to let the Jewish people decide. And perhaps the one place where we should draw a line is at the DIY bris!

Plugging In and Powering Up: Taking Advantage of Technology's Gifts

Growing up in Teaneck, New Jersey, in the 1950s, my dad's family was pretty religious – not quite Orthodox, but what we'd call today "Conservadox," meaning his family kept Shabbat and kosher, but didn't go to a synagogue where the men and women sat apart.

Like most kids back then, my dad grew up loving baseball. But because his family kept Shabbat, he couldn't watch the baseball games when they were played on Saturdays. That was usually fine. However, for the most important games of the season, like the playoffs, my dad had a work-around so he wouldn't miss them.

On Friday afternoon before Shabbat would start, he would turn on the TV to the correct station, turn the volume all the way down, and place a towel over the TV. Then, the next day, as they returned from synagogue, he would "accidentally" bump into the TV and the towel would just so happen to slide off the TV and fall to the ground. And what do you know – the game just so happened to be on!

My dad told me he and his buddies would also sneak their small, portable transistor radios into Sunday school. They'd snake their single earphone wire through their jacket sleeves and they'd all sit with their heads resting on one hand so the teacher didn't know what was going on. He said it usually worked beautifully until their team made a great play and all the boys in the class spontaneously burst into cheers, seemingly for no apparent reason.

I'm willing to bet that young Jews have been cleverly coming up with work-arounds for Jewish prohibitions since the beginning of time. It's likely that the *eruv* was dreamt up by a group of ten-year-old boys who wanted to play ball on Shabbat and needed to find a way to carry their ball to the empty lot just outside of town!

I have to give credit to the Reform movement for their efforts over the years to merge contemporary life with ancient traditions. According to the Central Conference of American Rabbis (the Reform rabbinic leadership organization),

> Reform rabbis integrate a Jewish dimension into contemporary life, providing an authentically Jewish voice, teaching Jewish values and traditions, and shaping the future. Since its founding in 1889, the Central Conference of American Rabbis has produced formal and informal statements that interpret the voice of prophetic Judaism, and that govern, guide, and express the contemporary views of the rabbinate.[12]

The Reform movement has a long history of coming up with creative solutions to modern problems, which even includes embracing technological advances. However, they are not too quick to embrace all technology to the point of tossing out tradition altogether. For example, the question of whether a minyan via the internet is kosher prompted a long back-and-forth quoting Torah and Talmud and various sages from different time periods. But in the end, they concluded:

---

12. "Rabbinic Voice," *Central Conference of American Rabbis*, last modified July 16, 2020, https://www.ccarnet.org/rabbinic-voice/.

> Whether through dial-in, live-streaming, or video
> connection, it is a good thing to encourage those who
> cannot attend the synagogue to be "technologically
> present." Such persons, however, are not part of the
> minyan, because the minyan is the community of
> those [who] are truly present with us, that is, in the
> real (as opposed to virtual) sense of that term.[13]

This may be the proper Solomonic solution, as it splits the
figurative baby, but it may not be enough to keep Jewish life
relevant for the next generation. For example, when my father
passed away and I wanted to say Kaddish for him, I couldn't
make it to a minyan every day. I asked a local rabbi about a
virtual minyan, but he told me that wouldn't be considered
kosher. So, I found a way to say Kaddish that worked for me,
but I wonder if it's time for that prohibition to fade away.

I asked the rabbi if a Jew in Juneau, Alaska, who couldn't
find a minyan would feel the same way. Maybe they would feel
the need to join a minyan virtually to say Kaddish and would
want it to be kosher. Maybe the inability for Judaism to address
that need would drive them away from Jewish life, and I asked,
"Wouldn't that be a worse outcome?" The rabbi answered that
if that person thought Jewish life was so important to them,
they wouldn't live in a place where there were no other Jews.

I didn't agree with him, and since the time of my father's
death, I've been stuck on this idea of a virtual Kaddish minyan.
It turns out that there is now a website called Kaddish.com,

---

13. CCAR Responsa Committee, "A Minyan via the Internet?" *Central Conference
    of American Rabbis*, last modified March 1, 2018, https://www.ccarnet.org/
    ccar-responsa/minyan-via-internet/.

which allows you to pay someone else to say Kaddish for you. I'm not sure of its validity since it was satirized in a brilliant and irreverent novel of the same name by Nathan Englander, but the website does seem to exist.

I continued to research the question because I still believe many Jews around the world who live in areas without easy access to a daily minyan might want to say Kaddish for a loved one regularly. In fact, they might want to say Kaddish with their own brothers, sisters, aunts, uncles, and cousins, even if those family members live far away and they're congregating in a virtual space. Ultimately, I found a number of apps that allow you to make a minyan at any time, anywhere in the world – but in real life, not in a virtual space. Here is a selection of some of them:

"**Minyan Now** lets you quickly create a minyan, a group of 10 Jewish males, wherever you may be, at any time of the day." This might be good if you're at the airport and need to pray, but it still requires you to be in-person. Oh, and this is only for men, so not very egalitarian.

"**TfilaFinder**. This application allows [you to] search minyans and shuls by location, by address and by time of day." This one might work if you're traveling and you want a traditional synagogue.

"**ShulTime** is an app to help people find a time to daven in a nearby Shul, Synagogue, or Minyan, within a specific area or city or zip by map...." This one also seems similar to the previous one – still no opportunity for a virtual minyan, though.

"**Minyan Maven** provides up-to-date details of the various *minyanim* in Melbourne, Australia and now Ramat Beit Shemesh Aleph, Israel." This one is very geographically specific. No wonder it only has one review.

YidKit includes a "Minyan Finder," which states: "Find *minyanim* near you, or search by zip code. View the minyan's info, contact information, and times." This one at least has a clever name, but again, it's only for an in-person minyan.

And, finally, there is indeed **Kaddish Assistant**, which among its many benefits, allows you to "Notify friends and loved ones when and where you will be saying Kaddish so they can join you and help you make a minyan." Closer, but still no ability to say Kaddish with a virtual minyan.

I am only spending so much time on the virtual minyan example to make a larger point, which is this: I don't know what the future holds for technology and science. But I know the combination of those two alchemies will surely come up with brilliant solutions to the world's biggest problems – from climate change to massive refugee resettlement to global hunger to catastrophic pandemics – and if the Jews are not willing to embrace science and technology to solve our own challenges, then we will seem archaic, unreasonable, and downright backwards to the next generation.

Yes, Judaism must maintain certain guardrails, otherwise at some point it fails to continue to be Judaism. But guardrails should be adjusted over time. When roads widen, guardrails must be moved to make room for more travelers. This is one of the central debates between the different denominations within Judaism, of course: where the guardrails around Jewish laws and customs should be placed, how liberally they should be adjusted, and whether to follow the spirit of the law or the letter of the law when interpreting them.

Today we are accomplishing what we thought was impossible only twenty years ago, such as uploading, cataloguing, and cross-referencing every single Jewish text on the internet thanks to Sefaria. What else will science allow Jews to do in the future? What other problems will science solve for the Jewish People? What will be considered going too far? And will the arbiters of Jewish law allow us to accept those solutions?

For Jewish Peoplehood to maintain its relevance and meaning for the next century, we must embrace the advances in science and technology that at one time seemed to come out of a science fiction novel but are now at our fingertips. We must be more aggressive in moving the guardrails to adapt to our twenty-first century realities, or we risk Judaism becoming completely out of touch for the vast majority of the Jewish People.

5

TACHLIS, A New Framework for Jewish Living

I didn't grow up in a religious family. However, I would argue that my family was indeed very Jewish. As I mentioned, we had Shabbat dinner every Friday night, but we didn't keep the Sabbath in the traditional sense. I went to Hebrew school, but we didn't go to synagogue other than twice a year, on Rosh Hashanah and Yom Kippur. (I've since learned that I grew up as an "H2O Jew": High Holidays Only.)

I didn't know that Jews prayed three times a day. I couldn't tell you what the Five Books of Moses were. And I never built a *sukkah* growing up. However, I felt deeply Jewish. Pastrami on rye, chopped liver, knishes, and Dr. Brown's Cream Soda was my food. Comedy from Carl Reiner, Mel Brooks, Gilda Radner, and Sid Caesar was my humor. *Yentl*, *Exodus* and *The Frisco Kid* were my movies. "Oy vey," "putz," and "schmuck" were my words.

I suppose today we'd call out the non-Jews who drop Yiddish into their daily lexicon as "culturally appropriating," but it's become so accepted by mainstream America to eat Jewish food and use Yiddishisms that the winning word for the Scripps National Spelling Bee in 2013 was "knaidel," the

Yiddish word for a matzah dumpling. Back when I was a kid, I didn't care if other people ate our food, laughed at our comedians, watched our movies, and spoke our words – as long as they knew it was *ours* first. I was proud of my heritage. I was the kid whom the teacher asked every year to explain Hanukkah and Passover to the rest of the class. (Thank God I was never asked to explain Shemini Atzeret.) I was the kid who chose to present on Masada in sixth grade – though for the life of me, I don't remember why. And I was the kid who dressed up as Elie Wiesel (in his later years) to teach my class about the Holocaust.

But growing up Jewish also meant living with a number of limitations. As I mentioned, we couldn't eat pepperoni pizza in the house, and my father wouldn't let us own a German shepherd or a German car either. (He continued for years to insist that his Audi was Swedish.) On certain days of the year, we couldn't go to school because of Jewish holidays. Come to think of it, that last one might have seemed like more of a gift than a limitation.

Even though I didn't know much about Jewish law or the restrictions that come with being Orthodox, I knew that being Jewish was a lot about what Jews could not do. I knew that observant Jews couldn't drive on Shabbat or even turn on the lights. I knew that Jewish women had to dress modestly, and that observant Jewish men couldn't even shake hands with women other than their wives. So, when I was young, despite my Jewish pride, I thought that being an observant Jew was a lot about what you couldn't do.

Additionally, I grew up as a proud Zionist, but I was always taught that Israel was our insurance policy. If, God forbid, there would ever be another Holocaust, Israel will be there to take us in. I took tremendous pride in the Israeli army that saved Jews in Ethiopia, Yemen, and Entebbe, and I knew if the antisemites ever came for us, Israel would save us too. But I didn't learn about modern Israeli culture. I didn't learn about Israel's diverse political make-up. And I definitely didn't learn Hebrew.

Now, I'm convinced that leading a meaningful Jewish life has to involve going deeper than feeding our kids cholesterol-rich food and introducing them to self-depricating comedians who have complicated relationships with their mothers. It has to be rooted in our values and be multi-layered, thoughtful, and intentional. It has to reach us where we are and engage all Jews in a way that speaks to them. It has to offer many portals of entry and be accessible for everyone, no matter what their starting point. Finally, it has to be action-oriented, as Judaism is so much more fulfilling when one embraces *doing* it.

I have a model for how to promote that type of Jewish life, how to "plug in" Jews of all backgrounds to meaningful and joyous Jewish experiences, and how to make it relevant for any age. It's called TACHLIS.

TACHLIS is a Yiddish word that means "getting down to business." It is a great word that has no English equivalent – like many great Yiddish words – but I find it's the perfect word in many situations. Like when you're sitting in a meeting and people are just talking to hear themselves speak, you can jump in and demand, "Nu![1] Let's talk *tachlis*. What are we actually going to DO?"

---

1. "Nu?" is the Yiddish or modern Hebrew equivalent of "so?" but with a bit more of that Jewish impatience, such as, "Nu?! Tell us, already!"

TACHLIS also happens to be perfect for framing a new model for Jewish living, as it incorporates seven key elements – and seven, of course, is a very Jewish number. For instance, the week is seven days long; the menorah has seven branches; shivah (the mourning period) lasts seven days; there are seven Torah blessings, called *aliyot*, during Shabbat; and a traditional bride and groom have seven days of celebration. I will take you through each of them one at a time.

T Is for Tikkun Olam

In 2018, David Koren, the CEO of an Israeli non-profit organization, reached out to us at the OFJCC. He ran ERAN, which is a twenty-four-hour crisis hotline for Israelis struggling with depression, suicidal thoughts, loneliness, and other worries that plague people from time to time. David was struggling to find volunteers to answer the phones in the middle of the night, which was the most important time to be prepared for phone calls, and he had a brainstorm. He realized the middle of the night in Israel was the middle of the day in the US, and he knew that Silicon Valley was home to tens of thousands of Israeli expats.

When he called the JCC, he spoke to the staff of the Israeli Cultural Connections Department, who immediately understood what needed to happen. The staff put out a notice on social media to our Israeli community, and within twenty-four hours, one hundred people had volunteered to go through the training and become ERAN operators.

Over the course of the next two years, Israeli volunteers in Silicon Valley answered hundreds of phone calls from people suffering in Israel, truly helping to save lives. Then, in 2020, when COVID struck, people all over the globe began to suffer from depression, loneliness, and worse. Suddenly, Israelis in Silicon Valley began calling ERAN in the middle of the night, and it was volunteers living in Israel who answered the phone, able to provide help from all the way across the world. That's what I call karma – and it's just one example of how we do good, how we give back, and how we repair the world.

Tikkun Olam translates as "repairing the world." It is the term we use when talking about the need to make the world a better place, to leave it better than we found it. For many Jews, their Jewishness is defined by how they are repairing the world. This is sometimes called social action, social responsibility, social justice, or social impact, but they all essentially mean the same thing, which is that our Jewish ethos requires us to improve the world.

Rabbi Jonathan Sacks believes that repairing the world means standing up and doing what's right, taking a stand, protesting if we must, and bringing others along with us. In *Lessons in Leadership*, he writes:

> It is not enough to be righteous if that means turning our backs on society that is guilty of wrongdoing. We must take a stand. We must protest. We must register dissent even if the probability of changing minds is small. That is because the moral life is a life we share with others. We are, in some sense, responsible for the society of which we are a part. It is not enough to be good. We must encourage others to be good.[2]

---

2. Rabbi Jonathan Sacks, *Lessons in Leadership: A Weekly Reading of the Jewish Bible* (Jerusalem: Maggid Books, 2015), 12.

The idea that Tikkun Olam is an essential aspect of Jewish identity is widespread within the progressive Jewish community. In fact, there's an old joke about a group of American Jews who travel to Israel and ask their Israeli host, "How do you say Tikkun Olam in Hebrew?" In each generation, the progressive Jewish community in America takes up an important cause in the name of Tikkun Olam. For example, in the 1960s during the civil rights movement, many Jews marched hand in hand with leaders like Martin Luther King, Jr., to show they could be a light unto the nations. Twenty years later, freeing Soviet Jews was an animating force for the American Jewish community to repair the world. Twenty years after that, fighting for LGBTQ rights catalyzed young, progressive Jews all over the country to take up that cause as a way to make the world a better place.

In 2019, one of the major emphases of those in our community seeking to do their part for Tikkun Olam was in the area of gun control. Deaths from gun violence were on the rise and several high-profile mass shootings at schools mobilized young people around the country to march, protest, and call for change. In 2020, a great deal of emphasis was placed on racial justice as a core element of Tikkun Olam, since the killing of unarmed black men in America reached harrowing proportions. Many young people, including young Jews, devoted energy, time, and money to fixing this brokenness. Environmental justice is another animating cause for young, progressive Jews looking for a way to fix a broken world today.

What's been interesting to observe is that for many of these young American Jews, taking up a social justice cause is helping shape their identities. Their sense of who they are in the world is being formed by the activism they choose to pursue, and this identity formation may or may not take on an overtly Jewish flavor. Some Jewish leaders are working hard to create that linkage, however. I know teachers and administrators at Jewish day schools, rabbis and cantors at synagogues, and counselors and advisors in Jewish youth groups who want to ensure that when Jewish kids take up a social justice cause – whether that cause is Jewish or not – the kids know they're engaging because their Jewish soul is calling on them to do so.

For example, at my children's school, Gideon Hausner Jewish Day School, the leadership is very intentional about ensuring the students' Jewish identity is connected to their Tikkun Olam instincts. The seventh graders choose a nonprofit organization to research, then raise money for it, and ultimately present to the class. It's called their "Avodah L'olam" project, which means "Work for the World." My son Elie chose HIAS, the Hebrew Immigrant Aid Society, which helps immigrants and refugees around the world because just as we were once strangers in a strange land, we are compelled to "Welcome the stranger. Protect the refugee." Because the school doesn't restrict who the students can support, some of his classmates chose non-Jewish organizations. But at the end of the day, the teachers made sure the kids knew that whomever they were supporting, they were doing so because of the core Jewish value of Tikkun Olam.

In each generation, Tikkun Olam is a mobilizing force for Jews to express their Jewish values, and it takes a different form each time. But what doesn't change is the fact that as Jews, we have a prophetic light inside us. When we see injustice, we are driven to make things right.

Tikkun Olam can be the first path for Jews to do Jewish.

It can be the first portal of entry for someone embarking on a Jewish journey. And it can be the most accessible piece of someone's Jewish identity, as it doesn't really require any outward manifestations of Jewishness.

For example, you don't have to be a Jew to have a strong desire to repair the world, to donate to important organizations, or to volunteer for great causes. You can be a really good person with a really good heart and act on your instincts to make the world a better place without being Jewish, of course. I'm sure most of us know many people like that, in fact. So, it's obvious that just engaging in Tikkun Olam doesn't make you Jewish. But it's a good start – and it's an especially good start if you don't divorce the acts of repairing the world from other aspects of your Jewish identity. In the words of Natan Sharansky and Gil Troy in *Never Alone*: "Something is off when Jews divorce *tikkun olam* from their Jewishness. And something is off when Jews embrace *tikkun olam* instead of their Jewishness."[3]

My suggestion, therefore, is to embrace the Jewishness underlying your beliefs and actions that make the world a better place. I'm not suggesting this should lead you to only help with Jewish causes. On the contrary, you *should* help with non-Jewish causes. But when you engage in acts of Tikkun Olam, do not make your Jewishness a secret. Make it clear that you are helping *because* you are Jewish, because this ethos is deep inside you, because you have a Jewish soul that commands you to do this. Proudly declare it to anyone who will listen.

---

3.   Natan Sharansky and Gil Troy, *Never Alone: Prison, Politics, and My People* (New York: Hachette Book Group, 2020), 353.

I'll end with a story to illustrate this point. In 2017, Daniel Lurie, the founder and CEO of Tipping Point Community, was a keynote speaker at the San Francisco Jewish Community Federation's annual Day of Philanthropy. He was on a panel, and after he gave an impassioned speech for the need to end poverty and homeless in San Francisco, a member of the audience stood up and asked Daniel what he was doing *Jewishly* to make the world a better place. The tone of the question implied that because Tipping Point is a secular organization and that Daniel is a Jew, he ought to focus his energy on something solely Jewish.

Daniel respectfully but forcefully responded by saying that he leads Tipping Point precisely *because* he is Jewish. His Jewishness is what drives him to want to end poverty and homelessness for everyone. He doesn't shy away from who he is; he lets everyone know it. And yet, he also doesn't believe he ought to just help the Jews because he's Jewish.

Daniel's answer was a modern-day version of Rabbi Hillel's famous quote, "If I am not for myself, then who will be for me? And if I am only for myself, what am I? And if not now, when?"[4]

Tikkun Olam is an ideal way to fulfill the wisdom in this quote, and it's a beautiful first step in forging your Jewish identity. But it's just the first step. There are six others worth embracing, too.

---

4.   *Pirkei Avot* 1:14.

A Is for Art and Culture

In 2016, the OFJCC had the opportunity to take over the management of the café on our campus. I hadn't ever run a restaurant before so, for advice, I reached out to a member of our board who was an investor in a number of restaurants. One of the first things he told me was that I needed to figure out what kind of food we wanted to serve. Did we want to be a breakfast place; a coffee and pastry shop; a soup, sandwich, and salad bar; or something else?

I had a clear vision for the kind of restaurant it should be and what type of food we should serve. This was a JCC, so we needed to serve Jewish food; obviously we needed to open a Jewish deli.

The next person we engaged to help us with the menu (and the logo, branding, and interior design) was a parent from the preschool who worked at IDEO. She was trained in design thinking, so she took us through a highly creative process to come to some conclusions. One of her suggestions was to poll the community to see what they wanted in the café. That turned out to be a good idea, as we learned a lot from the surveys and interviews, including that folks had different ideas of what "Jewish food" was.

It turns out that American Jews, like me, thought of Jewish food as typical Jewish deli items like pastrami and corned beef, matzah ball soup, knishes, chopped liver, and of course big, fat pickles. Meanwhile, Israelis thought Jewish food was falafel, hummus, eggplant salad, and chopped Israeli salad. That was an eye-opening moment for me about the importance of culture in determining one's identity – and it helped me realize I needed to stop being so rigid in my own thinking.

Food, music, literature, art, film, language, humor, and collective customs make up what is considered a group's culture – and you can't overestimate how much it can help people connect to one another. Art and culture can be deep and profound. It can bring tears to your eyes as it stirs up memories. It can make you think of home or lost relatives. It can connect us to our past and our future.

Often art and culture can be a tool for helping connect people to their heritage and to each other. It can be an un-intimidating way to bring people into a conversation with a lower barrier to entry. For example, the Jewish Studio Project, an organization led by Rabbi Adina Allen to help people by merging art therapy with Jewish learning and spiritual practices, "innovates a new approach to Jewish creativity – one in which art is not just for artists and Jewish texts are not just for scholars."

Many JCCs, including the OFJCC, have a vibrant program to bring art and culture to the broader community. The 92nd Street Y has perhaps the best-known cultural arts program of any JCC in the United States. Their mission statement says they are "a world-class cultural and community center where people all over the world connect through culture, arts, entertainment and conversations."

Jewish museums are an example of another way we share art, culture, history, memory, and more. By at least one count, there are more than a thousand around the world, not counting the ones in Israel.[5] Each one of these museums tells a story

---

5. Diana Muir Appelbaum, "Why Are There So Many Jewish Museums?" *Mosaic*, February 9, 2016, https://mosaicmagazine.com/response/arts-culture/2016/02/why-are-there-so-many-jewish-museums/.

and asks the listeners to be witnesses, to not forgot, to pass it on to the next generation, and to stay connected to our people.

Jewish books are another example of how Jews can connect to our culture. From the dialogues of the Kuzari to the parables of Shalom Aleichem to the novels of Anita Diamant, Jewish literature provides a tangible way for many Jews to feel Jewish.

Finally, visual, performing, and musical art can all touch the soul in such a way that an audience that shares the experience together can form a sudden bond over a shared, sublime moment; all the more so if the experience elevates a shared memory of a common people, as it did for me the first time I saw Marc Chagall's tapestries in the Knesset.

Art and culture are another way Jews can connect to their Jewishness that has a very low barrier to entry. I encourage you to explore different kinds of Jewish art and culture, experience a variety of modalities and media, and experiment with types that come from a totally different part of the world than where you live. It may just enrich your own Jewish identity while futher connecting you to the entire Jewish People.

C Is for Community

On September 11, 2001, I was in bed asleep when my boss called to tell me to turn on the TV. I arose and turned on the news to see that a plane had flown into one of the World Trade Center Towers. I sat down and watched, not understanding what I was seeing. Of course, it became clear over the next hour what was taking place: America was under attack by terrorists who were using airplanes as guided missiles.

Somehow, my living room became the gathering place for

my friends that day. People came and stayed for hours, unannounced, uninvited, but absolutely appreciated. We all sat and watched the TV all day long. We were in San Francisco, but we all had family or friends in New York and Washington, D.C. We didn't know if they were okay, as we couldn't reach them. And we didn't know what was happening with our country. Simply put, we didn't know anything except that a whole lot of people were hurting badly, including us.

All we could do at that moment was rely on each other. We cried with each other. We debated with each other. We consoled each other. We pontificated with each other. And ultimately, we were there for each other. Our little community of friends helped each and every one of us get through that terrible day.

Community is central to who we are as human beings. We are all searching for connection, for belonging. We are hardwired to seek community. And as Jews, we've built this into our operating system.

From the very beginning, God says, "It's not good for man to be alone."[6] The traditional Jewish way of learning is in a *chevruta*, a partnership with at least one other person. And to recite certain prayers, we need a community of at least ten – a minyan – to bring forth the Divine presence, to make the act holy.

Finding the right community can actually give your life meaning. It can have life-changing implications. It can influence your physical health: think about a cycling group, hiking club, or sports team. It can impact your mental health: when you are depressed, suffering a loss, or dealing with loneliness,

---

6.   Genesis 2:18.

your community can pull you up from the depths. It can even raise up your spiritual well-being. Rabbi Jonathan Sacks writes, "Community is the human expression of Divine love."[7]

Growing up, I felt most connected to my friends at Jewish summer camp. I didn't see them over the course of the year, but when I saw them during the summer, I was able to connect in a deeper and more genuine way than with my friends back home. I wasn't trying to be someone else at camp; I wasn't hiding anything. On the last night of camp one year, as we passed around the candle and all spoke about something we were going to miss when we left, I said I was going to miss how at home I felt with this group.

Camp is one of the greatest creators of community. Jewish summer camp allows the blossoming of friendships that last a lifetime, starting at a young age. Israel trips and youth groups also create tight communities for teens and young adults right at those moments when they're looking for their own sense of belonging.

These days, we talk about micro-communities, as it can be incredibly fulfilling to have a small group of people on whom to rely, with whom to celebrate and study, and to whom you can turn in the difficult moments as well. American liberal synagogues in the late '60s launched the "havurah move-ment" to create such micro-communities,[8] and I know many families that are still close to the members of their havurah. Today, organizations like Kevah are attempting to recreate

---

7.   Rabbi Jonathan Sacks, *Celebrating Life* (New York: Bloomsbury USA, 2019), 149.

8.   Jonathan Sarna, "Havurah Judaism" *My Jewish Learning*, last modified January 15, 2019, https://www.myjewishlearning.com/article/havurah-judaism/.

that same feel with small learning groups that meet in individuals' homes.

Charles Vogl, the author of *The Art of Community*, defines a community as "a group of individuals who share a mutual concern for one another's welfare."[9] That's what Jews are. That's what Jews do. When I was sitting shivah for my dad, plenty of people whom I knew came to pay respects, but many others came whom I didn't know. Some were newer friends of my dad's whom I never met, and others were just members of the synagogue who came to do a good deed. Each of those guests helped ease the pain just a little bit.

Finding the right community is central to living a meaningful Jewish life. Whether it's a Torah study group from your synagogue, or your Burning Man camp, this group can be there for you when you're searching. Whether it's a group of moms who met when their kids were in Jewish preschool together, or a regular yoga class at the JCC, this group can become your support network when you need a hand.

Philosopher Micah Goodman makes the case that belonging to a community can give your life meaning and vice versa. In his book *The Wondering Jew*, he states:

> There is a deep link between belonging and meaning. People who feel they belong to something greater than themselves sense that their lives are more meaningful. But modern life in the Western world, which induces people to become increasingly preoccupied

9. Charles Vogl, *The Art of Community: Seven Principles for Belonging* (Oakland, CA: Berrett-Koehler Publishers, 2016), 9.

with themselves, hampers their ability to feel they belong to anything, and therefore, threatens their sense that their lives have meaning.[10]

Building community is key to living a meaningful Jewish life. And if it's the first thing you embrace from the TACHLIS model, it will be a good start.

H Is for Holidays and Rituals

When I was a junior in high school, my soccer team was invited to play in a very prestigious soccer tournament called the Dallas Cup. This was an opportunity not to be missed. The problem was the tournament took place right smack in the middle of Passover. Because we needed a few parent chaperones and my father always loved to watch my soccer games, he joined me for the tournament in Dallas.

Despite my father and I being experts at "Jewish Geography," we didn't know anyone in Dallas. We had no friends or family that could even connect us to someone in Dallas. So my dad contacted the local synagogue and asked if they could find us a place to go for Passover Seder. Sure enough, they connected us to a nice family that opened their home to us and invited us to join their family's Seder.

My memory of that Passover is very hazy. I remember missing the rest of my family, and I'm sure it wasn't the same without Charlton Heston's voice to put me to sleep after my four cups of Manischewitz, but in the end, it was a Passover

---

10. Micah Goodman, *The Wondering Jew: Israel and the Search for Jewish Identity* (New Haven: Yale University Press, 2020), 40.

Seder like our people had been doing forever. And just as our people have done for thousands of years, a stranger opened his door to invite us to sit at his Passover table.

Holidays

Holidays are vital for marking the passage of time without just allowing it to move on without meaning. Holidays allow us to take stock of the current moment, especially as it relates to a previous moment. Holidays allow us to remember – remember our history, our stories, our family members, and our collective past. Holidays allow us to celebrate the wonderful and commemorate the tragic. Holidays allow us to connect to our ancestors and our descendants, knowing they too have engaged and will engage in similar ways as we are in that very moment. Holidays are the knots in the thread that connects us together over the generations.

One of the best ways to celebrate our holidays is simply by following the Jewish calendar. Rabbi Alan Lew in his book *This Is Real and You Are Completely Unprepared*, discusses the brilliance of the Jewish calendar. He reminds us that it is not just tied to the sun, like the Roman calendar, or the moon, like the Muslim calendar, but "the Hebrew calendar is the only one in the world that is both lunar and solar."[11]

By combining the solar and the lunar, the Jewish calendar marks the passage of time in a way that tracks to the seasons of the earth along with the seasons of our soul. What I've

---

11. Rabbi Alan Lew, *This Is Real and You Are Completely Unprepared: The Days of Awe as a Journey of Transformation* (New York: Little, Brown, and Co., 2003), 35.

found is that each Jewish holiday can be tied to a specific Jewish value, one that we can embrace in that moment and that can be taught to our children in that moment. If one looks at the months of the calendar and maps them to the holidays and then to specific values, you can live a Jewish year with meaning and purpose.

If you'd like to see what it's like to live a full year experiencing every Jewish holiday – from the most popular to the least known – I encourage you to read *My Year of Living Jewishly* by Abigail Pogrebin. But if you are looking for an abridged roadmap for beginners, here is an example of what it could mean to live a Jewish year from a minimalist perspective, choosing one holiday per month. Of course, the Hebrew months do not coincide with the English months perfectly, as it may seem below. But since this is a rudimentary road map for those wanting to begin a Jewish journey using holidays as their mile markers, I'm overlaying the months from the separate calendars for simplicity and ease of translation.

Month: September
Hebrew Month: Elul
Holiday: Rosh Hashanah and Yom Kippur
Value: *Cheshbon Hanefesh* (Self-Reflection and Self-Improvement)

The Jewish new year begins in the fall with Rosh Hashanah, which translates as "head of the year," so we embrace this month as a time to prepare by looking back and, simultaneously, looking forward. The values we want to celebrate this month are self-reflection and self-improvement. They come from reflecting on the past year, apologizing for the wrongs we committed, then forgiving ourselves (and others), wiping the slate clean, and starting over. At the same time, we want to look to the future, visualize where we want to be, and set goals for the coming year. These values, thoughts, and actions are two sides of the same coin, and they are epitomized by the holidays of Rosh Hashanah and Yom Kippur.

Month: October
Hebrew Month: Tishrei
Holiday: Sukkot
Value: Tikkun Olam (Repairing the World)

Sukkot is the Harvest Festival, a time to be grateful for our gifts and help those less fortunate. Whether for the roof over our heads or the food on our table, this is a time to appreciate our bounty. We show appreciation by putting up a temporary dwelling that is quite vulnerable to the elements called a *sukkah*, where we eat and may even sleep for the week. The fragile nature of these *sukkahs* (*sukkot* in Hebrew) brings us closer to nature and the environment that provides the gifts that sustain us. A wonderful way to show gratitude for what we have is to help those who don't have food to eat or a place to live. These acts of helping those less fortunate are how we make the world a better place, engaging in Tikkun Olam.

Month: November
Hebrew month: Cheshvan
Holiday: Shabbat
Value: Taking time to unplug,
unwind, relax, and be with family

So, it turns out that there are no Jewish holidays in the month of Cheshvan. But luckily, we have a holiday we celebrate every week: Shabbat. Shabbat, of course, is celebrated every Friday night and Saturday, and it is one of the core values Jews hold most dear. In fact, it is the only "holiday" mentioned in the Ten Commandments – so it's pretty darn important. In our ever-increasingly fast-paced world, where our phones are virtually cemented to our ears, we need to take some time to unplug. We need to recharge our *own* batteries. We need to relax, reflect, and spend time with family or friends. In the month of November, we have four Shabbats in which we can embrace this notion of unplugging.

Month: December
Hebrew month: Kislev
Holiday: Hanukkah
Value: *Tzelem Elohim* (We are all
created in God's image; Pluralism; Diversity)

The Hanukkah story is the quintessential story of religious pluralism. The miracle of Hanukkah is the story of a small band of believers withstanding the onslaught of a massive army trying to kill or convert them. When the Greeks attempted to destroy the Jews around 170 BCE, the Maccabees fought back. They stood up against religious tyranny, defending their faith. Hanukkah, the Festival of Lights, is a great time to appreciate how we are all made in God's image, how diversity and pluralism bring so much light into our lives. This may be an excellent opportunity for you to explore how Jews of different backgrounds, religiosities, or cultures celebrate Judaism. You may want to watch movies, read books, and visit places that will expose you to the beautiful mosaic of the Jewish People.

Month: January
Hebrew month: Tevet
Ritual: Havdalah
Value: Separation; Sacredness

The only Jewish holiday in Tevet (aside from the final days of Hanukkah) is the fast on the Tenth of Tevet – which commemorates the beginning of the siege of Jerusalem by the Babylonians. Since few outside the Orthodox community commemorate this fast day, it is a great time to embrace the concept of Havdalah. Havdalah is the short ceremony we do to acknowledge when Shabbat ends and the new week begins. *Havdalah* means "differentiation," and we use this ceremony to differentiate between the holy and the profane, the everyday and the special. This being the beginning of a new year according to the Roman calendar, it is a good time to consider how this coming year will be different than the last. Many people set new year's resolutions. Make sure to spend some time bringing the sacred into your life this month.

Month: February
Hebrew month: Shevat
Holiday: Tu b'Shevat
Value: Environmentalism

Tu b'Shevat is the "Birthday of the Trees," according to what my youngest child, Orly, told me she learned in Jewish preschool. It's Judaism's hat-tip to environmentalism. This holiday gives us a chance to more intentionally respect nature and the world that sustains us. We should honor our natural world by planting a tree in Israel (or anywhere, for that matter) or growing a garden in our backyard or our urban neighborhood. We should start to recycle, or if we do that already, then we should redouble our efforts and add composting to our routine. We should go out for weekly hikes (or snow hikes, considering the weather). Whatever we do, we should do more to show our respect for Mother Nature.

Month: March
Hebrew month: Adar
Holiday: Purim
Value: *Kehillah* **(Community)**

Purim is the one Jewish holiday in which the story does not mention God. It's a story of the peoples' triumph. But part of what made the Jews vulnerable in the first place was the fracturing of the Jewish community in the story – part of what made Queen Ester successful was her reliance on the Jewish community that reunited behind her. So, we commemorate Purim by engaging in four acts that we are commanded to do as a community: 1) tell the Purim story; 2) give gifts to each other; 3) provide food for the needy; 4) party like it's 1999! In fact, we are commanded to get so drunk that we can't tell the difference between Mordechai (Queen Ester's uncle) and Haman (the King's evil advisor). We could all use a little more fun in our lives, so this month we should really focus on the celebrating – and doing it with community.

Month: April
Hebrew month: Nisan
Holiday: Passover
Value: Freedom and Liberty

A traditional Passover Seder can leave one of the most indelible marks on a child's Jewish memory. It's when we come together as a family to tell the story of the Jews' exodus from Egypt, our journey from slavery to freedom. And we tell the story with serious style: blood and frogs, locusts and boils, death and miracles. Jewish ritual doesn't get any better than a good Passover Seder. But the underlying message of liberation has been adopted over the years for a variety of worthy causes. The civil rights movement used the story to showcase their fight for freedom, as did the Soviet émigré movement. So did the movement for women's equality, the LGBTQ rights movement, and many others. What are you fighting to liberate today? What freedoms do you want to more deeply appreciate? Perhaps there are more mundane enslavements we face today – like your cell phone or your paycheck. Whatever it is, let's use this time of renewal and rebirth (it is the beginning of spring too, remember) to free ourselves from something that ties us down.

Month: May
Hebrew month: Iyyar
Holiday: The "Yomim" (days) – Yom Hashoah,
Yom Hazikaron, and Yom Haatzma'ut
Value: Memory

Jews spend a lot of time remembering. We wrote the book on memory. Memory plays such a prominent role in our heritage, and this month of the Yoms is a great time to honor that value. Yom Hashoah commemorates the Holocaust, Yom Hazikaron commemorates those who died fighting for the State of Israel, and Yom Haatzma'ut, Israeli Independence Day, commemorates the establishment of the State of Israel. Rabbi Jonathan Sacks writes, "Jews were commanded, as it were, to become a nation of storytellers.... There is a fundamental difference between history and memory. History is 'his story,' an account of events that happened sometime else to someone else. Memory is my 'story.'"[12] Let's use this month to honor our past, to remember those who came before us, to learn a little of our story, and to pass it on to our children.

Month: June
Hebrew month: Sivan
Holiday: Shavuot
Value: Learning

Jews are the People of the Book. On Shavuot, we celebrate having received our Book, the Torah, on Mt. Sinai by staying up all night and studying Torah. What better way to show our appreciation for our Great Book then by having a month to celebrate reading, studying, and learning? Use this month to think seriously about learning, with a specific focus on literacy. You can teach a child to read or donate a book to a family. You can take your kids to the library and help them sign up for their first library card. You can start a book club with friends or begin taking a regular Torah or Talmud study class. You may also want to do more to show appreciation for teachers and educators. Or perhaps you can donate to an organization helping promote literacy like the Jewish Coalition for Literacy or PJ Library.

---

12. Rabbi Jonathan Sacks, *Lessons in Leadership* (Jerusalem: Maggid Books, 2015), 277–88.

Month: July
Hebrew month: Tammuz
Holiday: It's summer break,
so no holidays this month
Value: Israel

July is the ideal month to celebrate Israel. Why? First, it's the middle of summer so most kids are out of school, which means it's a perfect time to travel to Israel. Second, the only holiday in the month of Tammuz is the Fast of Tammuz, which commemorates the three weeks of mourning leading up to Tisha b'Av, when the Temple was destroyed. And where was the Temple located – in Jerusalem, the eternal capital of Israel! Israel is a central part of Jews' identity and has been since the beginning. So, take this month to learn a little bit more about Israeli culture and Israeli life.

Month: August
Hebrew month: Av
Holiday: Tu b'Av
Value: Joy and Love

While the traditional community identifies the month of Av more closely with elements of mourning the destruction of the Temple, there is one little-known holiday that celebrates love and joy during this month too. Tu b'Av is not widely celebrated outside Israel. But inside Israel and in some communities in the US where there are many Israeli expats, Tu b'Av is celebrated as the "Jewish Valentine's Day," a day to celebrate love. Historically, it marked the beginning of the grape harvest when unmarried young women would dress in white and dance in the vineyards. So, use this month to embrace the ideals of joy and love.

This roadmap for the holidays is just a suggestion for how to celebrate our heritage and mark the moments of transition throughout the year. It is not meant to be the authoritative calendar. I encourage you to explore the opportunities presented to us from our tradition and experiment with them as you go along your path. The one thing I urge you to do, however, is to know the basics. If you don't know the basics, it's hard to innovate off of them. There's one story in particular that comes to mind.

One of the boys who played on my son's soccer team was Jewish. Both his parents were Jewish. They were well-educated doctors who grew up in Jewish homes. They knew the importance of raising their children with a sense of their Jewishness, so they were members of a local synagogue.

One spring day, I was talking to the boy's father about the JCC's plans to commemorate Yom Hashoah, and he looked at me blankly. I could tell he didn't know when Yom Hashoah was, so I shared the date with him. When the *asimon* still didn't drop (an Israeli idiomatic expression for "didn't make the connection"), I told him that Yom Hashoah was Holocaust Memorial Day. With that clarifier, he nodded. Of course, he knew about the Holocaust. But he confessed to me that he never knew there was a holiday to commemorate it.

I was surprised. This well-educated Jewish adult who cared enough to be a member of a synagogue and send his child to Hebrew school – and by the way, his synagogue in particular holds an annual Yom Hashoah commemoration event – did not even know about the holiday at all. The Holocaust was the worst tragedy to befall our People since our enslavement in Egypt, and he didn't know that we have a day to memorialize it. It would have been one thing if he hadn't known about Yom

Hazikaron, the holiday when we commemorate Israel's fallen soldiers. I wouldn't expect every non-Israeli Jew to know about that holiday. But this was Yom Hashoah!

The thing is – I don't think he is alone. I bet many American Jews don't know we have a holiday to commemorate the Holocaust, and I wonder how many other holidays on my list are not known by a majority of the non-traditional Jewish population. Most Jews know the big four holidays: Rosh Hashanah, Yom Kippur, Hanukkah and Passover. But the other holidays are important as well. They are vital to helping us remember the story of the Jewish People, and making us feel connected to each other, tying the knots in the thread that connect our past to our future.

Rituals

Like holidays, rituals can also have deep meaning. Rituals can actually bestow meaning on profane moments. Rituals can mark the moments of transition that could otherwise pass without notice. Just as we do the calendar well, Jews do rituals well, too. Rabbi Daniel Gordis says in *God Was Not in the Fire*, "Judaism uses ritual to create moments of holiness, brief interludes into which Jews can bring the presence of God."[13]

Whether it's rituals of birth or death, or coming of age and marriage, Jews have a ritual for many of the most important moments in our lives. We don't cover them all, however, so this may be one area where we can innovate. Professor Shaul

---

13. Gordis, *God Was Not in the Fire*, 111.

Magid calls the invention of new rituals "vibrant secular Judaism."[14]

Several years ago, at the OFJCC we wanted to inspire the creation of new rituals, so we put out an RFP for people to pitch their ideas to be awarded a micro-grant. We didn't receive many submissions, but one in particular won our approval and some money. The woman who submitted it was a family attorney, and she found that many of the women she represented in divorce cases felt they needed some sort of cleansing ritual to mark the moment, to allow them to put their past behind them, and to move on. She created a new divorce ritual that involved some prayers, readings, and a dip in the *mikvah*, the ceremonial bath.

Religious scholar Vanessa Ochs's book *Inventing Jewish Ritual* is a wonderful road map for those looking to be creative in this realm. She says, "Judaism is a dynamic, evolving tradition, one continuously sculpted by its loving practitioners. Jews keep Judaism alive through inventing new rituals – moving, fulfilling, and authentically Jewish rituals. More of us, I discovered, are poised to craft and embrace new Jewish rituals than we may realize."[15]

Sometimes it's not even reinventing a ritual so much as infusing new meaning into traditional rituals, or ritual objects. Barry Finestone, president of the Jim Joseph Foundation, shared with the board of the OFJCC that a traditional *mezuzah*

---

14. Shaul Magid, interview with Daniel Libenson and Lex Rofeberg, *Judaism Unbound*, podcast audio, May 13, 2016. https://www.judaismunbound.com/podcast/2016/5/6/episode-13-american-post-judaism-shaul-magid.

15. Vanessa Ochs, *Inventing Jewish Ritual* (Philadelphia: The Jewish Publication Society, 2007), 1.

can serve a contemporary purpose by delineating space and time. He recommended that as we come home from work, we should pause at our door before we fly right into the house and take a moment to look at the *mezuzah* to remind ourselves: I am leaving work outside and I am coming into a new space, so I can greet my family with love and a renewed sense of vigor.

How often do we bring our worst selves home because we are exhausted and worn out, and we don't take the time to dig deep and be patient with our spouses and kids the way we need to be with clients and coworkers? I know I do that way too often.

Ultimately, whether we celebrate holidays or rituals or both, the key is to do it with gusto, to dive in, and in many cases, to be joyous. Of course, not all holidays and rituals are meant to create joy. Periods of mourning, for example, are not meant to invoke joy. Celebrating Yom Kippur is another example of when we are not meant to by joyful – at least the entire time. Some of our most important holidays and rituals are meant to create moments of insight and self-reflection, which don't always start or end in a place of joy. Sometimes it's doing what we are commanded to do as Jews, since part of what it means to be a Jew is to live a life of commandedness. An example of how commandedness might fit within the TACHLIS model is engaging in the ritutal of *brit milah* (circumcision for an eight-day old Jewish baby boy) or sitting shivah (mourning for seven days after the death of a family member), both of which can be quite difficult to experience but can also add immeasurable meaning in the life of the observer of that ritual. Even in those moments, it's still possible to infuse the rituals with new meaning and relevance, which in the long run, can add up to a full life filled with purpose and joy.

Abraham Joshua Heschel says we must balance the *keva* (regularity) with the *kavanah* (intentionality) so we can get the most out of the experience.[16] So, whatever you do, make sure you give it your all.

L Is for Learning

During the winter of 1996, I spent a month studying at Ohr Somayach yeshiva in Jerusalem. It was a very traditional Orthodox learning center where the *beit midrash* (study hall) was filled with the voices of young men arguing and debating in traditional *chevruta*- (one-on-one-) style learning. In addition to engaging in *chevruta*-style study, I listened to lectures from visiting scholars, sat in on classes with esteemed rabbis, and engaged in informal discussion with other yeshiva *buchers* (young, male students at Jewish religious schools).

I loved learning about my heritage and hearing the stories that had been passed down for thousands of years. But when it came time to pray, I checked out. It didn't speak to me: I couldn't understand the language; I found the repetition of the same prayers over and over again uninspiring; and I didn't feel any elevation in my soul when I prayed. So, when they tried to get me to stay through Shabbat, I took off and went to Tel Aviv for the weekend, where I partied in the clubs and discos and crashed at my girlfriend's uncle's apartment.

That was the best of both worlds for me: studying during the week in Jerusalem, and partying on the weekends in Tel

---

16. Abraham Joshua Heschel, *Moral Grandeur and Spiritual Audacity* (New York: Farrar, Straus and Giroux, 1997), 113.

Aviv. I've since grown up a bit, which means I continue to study, but now I do a lot less partying.

Studying our ancient Jewish texts like the Torah and Talmud is key to knowing who we are as a People. It's essential that we know where we come from, who our great sages and heroes are, and the lessons that have shaped our history. Even a basic knowledge of these texts is crucial to understanding the beauty and wisdom in Judaism. I don't believe you have to be a Torah scholar, but having a grasp of the fundamentals is an important element of Jewish identity formation.

Yes, Jewish learning must include elements of our ancient texts, but it doesn't have to be limited to those. The full Jewish canon includes the stories of Cynthia Ozick and the poetry of Yehuda Amichai. It can include the philosophy of Martin Buber and the essays of Emma Lazarus. It can include the novels of Ruby Namdar and the comedy of Sarah Silverman. It can include Coen Brothers movies, Will Eisner comics, and Rashida Jones TV shows. It can include weekly podcasts from *Judaism Unbound* and videos from *BimBam*.

I see each of these elements as legitimate avenues of Jewish learning, and frankly, it shouldn't matter which path you choose – as long as you choose a path. Jewish learning is absolutely central to Jewish identity. You can't know who you are as a person unless you know the People to whom you're attached. Or in the more prophetic words that Danny Gordis once said to me, "If you want to architect the Jewish future, you need to study the Jewish past."

That line was captured from a conversation I had with Danny, but in his book, *God Was Not in the Fire*, he puts it just as powerfully in writing: "Jewish tradition even suggests that the only person who could merit even more respect than one's parent is one's teacher."[17] Jewish learning and literacy is core to who we are. The *heder* (a traditional Jewish elementary school classroom) has been key to our identity for hundreds of years, and that concept has only expanded over the generations. According to AVI CHAI's census of Jewish day schools in 2018–19, there were 906 day schools in the US that enrolled more than 292,000 children from kindergarten through twelfth grade.[18] Add to that the twelve Jewish universities and colleges in the US and you see why we are called "The People of the Book."[19]

Studying our great books, our collected wisdom, our history – or "memory", as Avraham Infeld would say – is a hallmark of Jewish life. My father-in-law says that his own father often told him, "Give me school over shul, any day." Meaning, it was the learning that inspired him Jewishly, not the praying. And I don't think he was alone.

Today, many Jewish organizations, including JCCs, have made Jewish learning core to what we do. We offer classes and lectures, of course, but we also offer what we call "cohort learning," which means we bring together a group of like-minded individuals to not only learn together and engage in social justice projects together, but to bond together as a group. We've witnessed that a group of separate individuals can come together and create a mutually caring micro-community

---

17. Gordis, *God Was Not in the Fire*, 58.
18. "A Census of Jewish Day Schools in the United States," AVI CHAI, accessed February 20, 2021, https://avichai.org/knowledge_base/a-census-of-jewish-day-schools-2018-2019-2020/
19. "List of Jewish universities and colleges in the United States," *Wikipedia*, last modified April 1, 2020, https://en.wikipedia.org/wiki/List_of_Jewish_universities_and_colleges_in_the_United_States.

among themselves when they learn together. At the OFJCC, we have cohorts of Israelis, women, budding philanthropists, and young professionals, just to name a few.

We also have a philosophy that collaboration is essential, as we don't have all the answers or all the tools. So, we partner with other institutions that are experts in Jewish learning like the Shalom Hartman Institute, BINA, 929, and Pardes, not to mention our local synagogues and institutions of higher learning like Stanford.

When it comes to where we offer learning at the JCC, we do it in and outside the building – in people's homes, on the hiking trail, at Napa wineries, and on the beaches. And of course, in the wake of COVID19, we offer learning on Zoom, through Facebook live, and Google Hangouts. Wherever we can inspire someone to learn, we will jump at the opportunity.

In the Mishnah it says, "Provide yourself a teacher and get yourself a friend."[20] In the TACHLIS framework, if you do that, then the learning will follow.

I Is for Israel

Growing up Jewish, in my home, meant growing up Zionist. My parents co-led one of the first international BBYO Teen Tours to Israel in the summer of 1974. My father remembered that trip to Israel – his first – as one of the seminal moments in his life. He wore Naot sandals, cutoff jeans and a *kova tembel* (the silly hat worn by kibbutzniks). He met Israeli soldiers and artists – often one and the same – and kept a truly ugly sculpture on his desk until he died that was a gift from one of

---

20. *Pirkei Avot* 1:6.

those artists. My father saw the results of the Yom Kippur War, and those images seared themselves in his mind.

I have two distinct classroom memories from my early years that relate to Israel.

When I was in third grade, Israel was in the midst of the Lebanon War. I was a student at a private school where my mom taught, so the teacher in my class was able to take certain liberties with the curriculum that a public school teacher might not have. For instance, although we were only eight-year-old kids, I remember him tacking up on the bulletin board articles clipped from the newspaper about the Lebanon War. The articles were invariably about Israeli atrocities, Israeli war crimes, and Palestinian victims of Israeli terror. I didn't understand anything about the conflict, and I surely didn't know anything about geopolitics, but I remember feeling really uncomfortable seeing those articles tacked up next to our class's self-portraits and "hopes and dreams."

Then, when I was a sophomore in high school, Israel was in the midst of the First Intifada. I remember seeing articles in the newspaper that came to my house every morning and asking my parents about the situation. I was curious, often asking obnoxious questions in that rebellious teen sort of way, but still felt a familial loyalty to the Jewish state – even if I couldn't explain why. Of course, we discussed the topic in class too, and I remember my world history teacher not generally accepting my defense of Israel's actions. He was always challenging me a little too aggressively. Then one day, he gave me his marked-up copy of Edward Said's book *The Question of Palestine* and told me to read it because it presented "a more accurate picture than what I'd been taught." Undoubtedly kids in school today are faced with even more challenging situations when it comes to their support of Israel, but back then this felt like a shot across the bow.

Then I finally took my first trip to Israel the summer after my junior year in high school – it was one of those eight-week teen tours – and the experience was transformative for me. To state the obvious: Israel was so different from the US – not only the intense heat and the Hebrew language and the bright light bouncing off the limestone – but in its expression of its Jewishness as well.

I remember being struck by the thought that every bus driver and janitor in Israel was Jewish[21] – which was definitely not the case in the US, where I naively imagined all Jews were white-collar professionals. I remember the pride I felt seeing young, beautiful Israeli soldiers, both men and women, in uniform with machine guns slung over their shoulders and thinking to myself, "We don't do Jewish power like that in the US." I saw graffiti scrawled across the walls in Hebrew and thought, "That's been done by Jewish hooligans. We don't have those in the US, either."

This was a Jewish experience I'd never had before – and I loved it. This was my place. These were my people. I was home.

There is only one Jewish homeland. Today we are blessed to be living in a unique moment in history when the State of Israel has been reborn. For nearly two thousand years, Jews ached, begged, prayed, and died to be able to return to Israel. And now we can.

Of course, Israel is not perfect. Show me one country that

---

21. I want to point out that I was young, so this was my naïve impression as a teenager.

is! Of course, many of us are going to disagree with its politicians, policies, and politics. Many Jews disagree with our own country's, as well. But that's not the point. The point is that we finally have our homeland back, and it's our job to protect it, to support it, to visit it, to learn about it, to engage with it, to wrestle with it, and to love it despite its flaws.

We must change the way we educate about Israel in America. On the one hand, for those critical of Israel, instead of focusing only on the areas where we take issue – like the occupation and the Chief Rabbinate – we must focus on the whole story. On the other hand, for those unable to see Israel's flaws, instead of sweeping them under the rug or ignoring them, we must shine a light on them so the next generation doesn't think we've lied to them. Educating about Israel takes creativity, knowledge, and nuance.

American comedian and actor Seth Rogen put his foot in his mouth during a podcast in July of 2020, in which he said, "I was fed a huge amount of lies about Israel my entire life."[22] He took some serious flak for his comment, some of which was clearly well deserved, but Danny Gordis said it best in his *Times of Israel* article when he wrote:

> Assuming that the Jewish education that Rogen received wasn't that different from ours or that of our children (even those who went to excellent Jewish high schools, by the way), Rogen's comment is eminently understandable. If we're taught that Israel is about keeping the Jews safe (especially after the Shoah) but

---

22. Seth Rogan, interviewed by Marc Maron, *WTF*, podcast audio, July 27, 2020. http://www.wtfpod.com/podcast/episode-1143-seth-rogen.

we also teach that Israel is constantly under attack, how much sense does Israel really make? If we're honest about how we teach our kids, it's hard not to feel badly for Rogen and the hot water in which he found himself.[23]

We need to teach Israel differently in America. We need to teach Israeli cooking, Israeli literature, Israeli art, Israeli politics, Israeli history, Israeli music, Israeli religiosity, Israeli social justice, and even the Israeli language – which is the true language of the entire Jewish People – Hebrew.

When we learn about Israel and Israelis, we will come to know the country and its people. We will be able to say we understand why and how the other exists. We will come to love and respect one another. And then, and only then, we will be able to argue effectively with each other about all those issues that drive us nuts because we'll engage in a healthy debate from a place of brotherhood, not animosity, and it will be as it was meant to be in the Talmud, a *mahloket l'shem shemayim*, an argument for the sake of heaven.[24]

23. Daniel Gordis, "What If Seth Rogen Wasn't (Entirely) Wrong?" *Times of Israel*, August 28, 2020, https://blogs.timesofisrael.com/what-if-seth-rogen-wasnt-entirely-wrong/

24. *Pirkei Avot* 5:17.

S Is for Shabbat and Spirituality

When I worked for AIPAC, I'd travel to Anchorage, Alaska once a year. I'd go and visit the "Frozen Chosen," as we called the handful of Jews up there. I'd speak at the local synagogue, schmooze with the Jewish community, and caucus with the political and legislative leaders as well.

In the early days of my visits to Alaska, I would go during the summer months when the weather was warmer and I could tack on a day for sightseeing. Eventually, I realized I couldn't see as many people as I needed to because I learned that the locals left town during the summer months for their cabins on one of the many islands outside of Anchorage. So, reluctantly, I began traveling to Alaska in the frigid months of October or November. And at least once, I went in February, when it was so cold that I couldn't be outside for more than half a second without my nose hairs completely freezing.

On one of my earlier trips when I went up during the summer, I brought a colleague, Elliot Brandt, who is Shabbat observant. That means during the Sabbath he won't drive, turn on electricity, or use money. Now if you know anything about Alaskan daylight cycles, you'll know that the sun doesn't set until eleven p.m. during the summer. Which means those who are Shabbat observant can't engage in any of those prohibited acts all day on Saturday.

So, on that particular trip, I recall clearly that in addition to having to walk to all of our meetings all day long, we had to make our eating plans the day before. We found a restaurant where we wanted to eat dinner on Saturday, so we approached the proprietor on Friday afternoon and explained the situation. Imagine it like a sort of like an Abbot and Costello routine:

Elliot: Do you have any tables available tomorrow night at eight p.m.?

Restauranteur: Yes, sir.

Elliot: Great. Can we please make a reservation for two people?

Restauranteur: Yes, sir.

Elliot: Wonderful. Can we order now, please?

Restauranteur: I'm sorry, sir. I don't understand. You want a table for two now?

Elliot: No. We want to come back here tomorrow night at eight.

Restauranteur: Okay. So why do you want to order now? The food will be quite cold.

Elliot: No. We don't want to eat it now. We want to preorder it now, but still eat it tomorrow night.

Restauranteur: So why don't you just order it tomorrow night, sir?

Elliot: Because we can't ask you to make the food tomorrow night.

Restauranteur: But you can ask us to make it tonight?

Elliot: Yes.

Restauranteur: So, you want us to make it tonight and bring it to you tomorrow night?

Elliot: No. We actually want you to make it tomorrow night, but we can't ask you to make it tomorrow night.

Restauranteur: You can't ask us to make it tomorrow night, but you can ask us to make it tonight?

Elliot: That's right.

Restauranteur: Okay, I suppose we can do that. I'll just put it in the system now.

Elliot: Great. Thank you. Can I pay you now?

Restauranteur: I'm sorry, sir, but you want to pay now?

Elliot: Yes, we want to pay now, with a tip and everything, so we won't get a bill tomorrow night or have to even think about paying tomorrow night.

Restauranteur: Let me guess: you can't ask for the check tomorrow night either, but you can ask for it tonight?

Elliot: Exactly.

Restauranteur: Okay, but you'll have to sign the check tomorrow night after we print it out.

Elliot: No, we'd rather sign the check now.

Restauranteur: But you haven't paid for anything because you haven't eaten anything. So why would you sign the check now?

Elliot: Because we can't handle money tomorrow...because it's the Jewish Sabbath...and we are not allowed to engage in commercial transactions on the Sabbath.

Restauranteur: Ok, sir. I suppose we can take care of this for you.

In the end, it was quite a memorable Shabbat for both of us, as I'd never celebrated a full Shabbat in the traditional way before, and he'd rarely spent time in a place where Shabbat ended at eleven o'clock at night!

Shabbat and Spirituality is the last leg of the TACHLIS framework. You can't lead a Jewish life if you haven't at least thought about Shabbat and spirituality. It doesn't mean you have to celebrate Shabbat in the traditional way – though I'd recommend celebrating some form of Shabbat. And it doesn't mean you have to engage in a regular spiritual practice – though again, I'd encourage searching for your own spiritual path.

Shabbat

Let's start with Shabbat. In Arthur Green's phenomenal little book *Judaism's 10 Best Ideas: A Brief Guide for Seekers*, he shares what he calls "the core of Jewish teaching, the ideas that represent the Jewish people's greatest ongoing contribution to human civilization."[25] And it should be no surprise that one of the "best ideas" presented in the book is Shabbat.

Like my own Alaskan experience, Green recognizes that many Jews today see Shabbat solely as a list of prohibitions. He says, "For many Jews entering the modern world, it all seemed so old-fashioned and repressive. The Sabbath was just a great list of 'don'ts.'"[26]

I can relate. As I mentioned earlier, growing up Jewish meant what I couldn't do – including not going out on Friday nights (though eventually, my father and I struck a deal on that one). My father also often complained that soccer games were on Saturdays. He would have much preferred them to be on Sundays so he could enjoy his Shabbat without running

---

25. Arthur Green, *Judaism's 10 Best Ideas: A Brief Guide for Seekers* (Woodstock, VT: Jewish Lights, 2014), 1.
26. Green, *Judaism's 10 Best Ideas*, 39.

around from city to city, game to game, rushing to ensure my brother and I were not late.

Arthur Green recognizes this is how Shabbat is seen too often today, but he pleads for us to look past these prohibitions. He says, "Shabbat is needed now more than ever. We Jews should be missionary about Shabbat. It may be the best gift we have to offer the world!"[27]

I couldn't agree more. I believe we could consider Shabbat the single greatest religious invention of all time. (That is, if we don't consider the concept of "God" a human invention, which I do not.) Shabbat is a gift for all living creatures, humans and animals, Jews and non-Jews. In a world that doesn't stop moving, it is permission to stop. At a time when progress is celebrated, Shabbat is a day of rest. In this moment when we are charging ahead, Shabbat is our license to catch our breath.

I repeatedly hear from non-Jewish preschool families at the OFJCC that they love Shabbat. Not only do they love coming to the classroom to watch their kids sing and express so much joy for the coming of the Sabbath, but they actually love the idea of a day to unplug, relax, and reconnect with family.

One story in particular stands out for me. I was meeting a couple who had their two children in our preschool. Neither of the parents was Jewish, and when I asked why they sent their kids to our preschool, they replied, "We love it here. The teachers love our kids, and we love the Jewish values. For example, we love Shabbat."

I asked if they meant Shabbat in the classroom, but they said, "Yes, and Shabbat at home too."

---

27. Green, *Judaism's 10 Best Ideas*, 40.

I asked them to explain, as I knew neither of them was Jewish. They said, "We now do a family dinner every Friday night. We cherish the time together as a family at the table. We put away our cell phones and we just engage with each other. It's the only meal all week that we make sure we are together for and that there is no tech at the table."

They went on to tell me they even take it one step further. The father said, "Last weekend, I took the kids on a camping trip and I made sure to come to the JCC beforehand so I could get my challah. My kids demand challah on Friday nights, so we ate it around the campfire."

A couple years later, after the kids had left our preschool, I caught up with the mother and asked if they were still doing Shabbat. She said they still are, but one of their kids had since been diagnosed with some severe food allergies, so they no longer buy their challah from the JCC. But now they are making homemade challah every Friday as a family as part of their family Friday night dinner tradition!

That's a perfect example of how a non-Jewish family can have a meaningful Jewish journey, can learn from Jewish values, and even incorporate Jewish rituals and holidays into their lives in a way that works for them. And there is no better holiday or ritual to start with than Shabbat.

Abraham Joshua Heschel says we should make Shabbat "a sanctuary in time."[28] As we spend most of our week sanctifying space, on Shabbat we must sanctify time. In his book, *The Sabbath*, he says Shabbat is an "echo of eternity,"[29] and asks,

---

28. Abraham Joshua Heschel, *The Sabbath* (New York: Farrar, Straus, and Giroux, 1951), 10.
29. Heschel, *The Sabbath*, 10.

if we can't learn how to enjoy one single day a week of peace, then how are we supposed to enjoy an eternity of peace in the world to come? Heschel declares:

> The meaning of the Sabbath is to celebrate time rather than space. Six days a week we live under the tyranny of things in space; on the Sabbath we try to become attuned to *holiness in time*. It is a day on which we are called upon to share in what is eternal in time, to turn from the results of creation to the mystery of creation; from the world of creation to the creation of the world...[30]

Heschel also flips the idea of Shabbat on its head. Rather than see Shabbat as a time to recharge ourselves so we can be refreshed and ready to go back to work at the beginning of the week – as most Westerners do – he suggests we see it the other way around. Heschel says the work week exists so we can celebrate Shabbat. Shabbat is the end, and the work week is the means, not the other way around.

In the twenty-first century, there is a great deal of talk about mindfulness as a response to the anxiety and pressure and "go-go-go" we all feel. Our children are facing "toxic stress" in schools, so much so that schools are beginning to implement mindfulness classes and teachings. One of the main themes of mindfulness is being in the moment and appreciating the present.

In *Practicing the Power of Now*, Eckhart Tolle says, "The eternal present is the space within which your whole life

---

30. Heschel, *The Sabbath*, 10.

unfolds, the one factor that remains constant. Life is now. There was never a time when your life was not now, nor will there ever be."[31] That is the key to mindfulness: appreciating the present. And that is what Shabbat is bringing to the fore-front for all of us who are focusing too much on the past or the future: be in the present.

Tolle goes on to say, "Presence is the key to freedom, so you can only be free now."[32] That's what Shabbat does – it sanctifies the now, the present moment, and gives us the ulti-mate freedom. Shabbat is the key to being free.

Today, we actually spend most of our time as "human doings," not "human beings," but Shabbat is our invitation to be "human beings" once again. We can just *be*, without any obligation to *do* anything.

In her book *24/6: The Power of Unplugging One Day a Week*, filmmaker and author Tiffany Shlain makes the case that we all need a day of rest, even if it isn't on the traditional Sabbath day and celebrated in the traditional way. For her and her family, they make it a tech-free Shabbat. So, it's not about refraining from using electricity or driving a car; they just stay away from screens because they feel that's the rabbit hole that keeps them from differentiating that day from the rest of the work week. This is a great example of how to take an ancient idea and blend it with the needs of a contemporary world, and come up with a hybrid solution.

Tiffany is a member of REBOOT, an "arts and culture nonprofit that reimagines, reinvents and reinforces Jewish

31. Eckhart Tolle, *Practicing the Power of Now* (Novato, CA: New World Library, 1999), 31.
32. Tolle, *Practicing the Power of Now*, 39.

thought and traditions." One of REBOOT's projects is the Sabbath Manifesto, "a creative project designed to slow down lives in an incredibly hectic world."

The Sabbath Manifesto promotes a "National Day of Unplugging" every year. They give out cell phone sleeping bags to encourage people to put their phones away on Shabbat. And they have a list of Ten Principles that everyone should strive to embrace on Shabbat:

1. Avoid technology
2. Connect with loved ones
3. Nurture your health
4. Get outside
5. Avoid commerce
6. Light candles
7. Drink wine
8. Eat bread
9. Find silence
10. Give back

I find this list easy to get my arms around and absolutely doable. It's not too onerous. It doesn't put me too much out of my comfort zone, but it still challenges me. And it doesn't feel at all archaic. So, for me, this is a perfect example of how to make Shabbat meaningful, relevant, and joyous for modern Jews. *Kol hakavod*, REBOOT!

I'll end my Shabbat shpiel with this final note. During COVID, when I and so many others began working from home, I found that I had a very difficult time differentiating space and time. The joke between my wife and I was, "Are we working from home or living at work?"

Often when I had a spare moment, no matter what day

or what time, I'd wander into my office, power up my laptop, and start to do work. It was bad enough that the spaces in my world became so intermingled, but now increasingly I had no division between the time in my life either. My work week and the weekend were sliding into each other. I felt like I was constantly working without getting a single day's break.

When I shared this with Tiffany Shlain, she urged me to recognize the power of Shabbat. She reminded me that my mind and body need the rest and that I will be a better father and husband – and CEO – if I take a day to unplug. She said that I wasn't doing myself any favors by working all the time.

I know she was right. I'm still not where I want to be in making Shabbat holy. But I am working on it. My goal is to be completely free from screens and technology one day a week. And from there, who knows?

Spirituality

Now, when it comes to the other part of the S in TACHLIS, spirituality, this is a bit tougher to capture in a few pages because it is highly personalized. But I believe for one to live a Jewish life, some spirituality must be involved. And there are plenty of options to choose from for how to do Jewish spirituality. I'll give one example here because I think it illustrates just how flexible Judaism can be in enabling individuals to express their spirituality.

Rabbi Amichai Lau-Lavie leads Lab/Shul, which is "an artist-driven, everybody-friendly, God-optional, pop up, experimental community for sacred Jewish gatherings based in NYC, reaching the world." According to their website, "Lab/Shul welcomes people of all races, religions, beliefs, gender expressions, sexual orientations, countries of origin, ages, abilities, families, and flavors with open hearts."

I've been to services at Lab/Shul; I've learned and prayed with Amichai; I've invited Amichai to speak at the JCC, and each time I've engaged with Amichai, I've been spiritually moved. The experiences remind me of my summer camp Shabbats, when I felt so connected to the beauty of the place, the joy in the songs, and the comradery of my friends. So, I can assure you that even with a spiritual leader who creates a space that is "God-optional" and an environment open to people of all beliefs, you can still have a deeply spiritual experience.

For what it's worth, you might recall from the first chapter that I am not God-optional. I do believe in God. But I believe in a more panentheistic view of God. That means that I believe that there is Divine presence in everything. The Great Spirit pervades the entire universe and goes beyond space and time. I believe God is in all things, and is indeed One. I strive to embrace the notion of the All-Beingness of God as Arthur Green describes it in his book *Radical Judaism* when he discusses mystical panentheism:

> There is no ultimate duality here, no "God and world," no "God, world, and self," only one Being and its many faces. Those who seek consciousness of it come to know that it is indeed *eyn sof*, without end. There is no end to its unimaginable depth, but so too there is no border, no limit, separating that unfathomable One from anything that is. Infinite Being in every instant flows through all finite beings.... When I refer to "God," I mean the inner force of existence itself, that of which

one might say: "Being is." I refer to it as the "One" be-cause it is the single unifying substratum of all that is.[33]

This belief allows me to see miracles in everyday life. I don't have to resign myself to miracles only happening in the biblical era, when Moses parted the Red Sea. Instead, I can appreciate that the birth of an animal that comes from two other animals is a miracle. I can appreciate that the ability for the eye to see and the nose to smell is a miracle. I can appreciate that the changing of the seasons, when plants and animals go into hibernation and then reemerge as if rebirthed, is a miracle. I can appreciate that the way our expelled breath gives life to plants and trees, which then turn that into the vital oxygen that gives us back life is a miracle.

Because I believe God is in everything, I am able, in my most attentive moments, to appreciate so much more of life. Of course, I'm not always so clear-eyed, but I strive to be more intentional about it every day.

One of the spiritual practices I've begun to incorporate into my life is Mussar. According to Greg Marcus in *The Spiritual Practice of Good Actions*, "Mussar can be translated from Hebrew to mean 'correction' or 'instruction.' In modern Hebrew, *Mussar* means 'ethics.' When we practice Mussar, which is essentially Jewish mindfulness, we are adjusting and correcting our soul – but we don't try to adjust the whole thing at once. Rather, we focus on specific parts of the soul called soul

---

33. Arthur Green, *Radical Judaism: Rethinking God and Tradition* (New Haven: Yale University Press, 2010), 18–19.

traits."[34] Mussar practice allows me to focus on soul traits like humility, patience, silence, equanimity, and gratitude.

Gratitude in particular plays an important role in my spiritual practice. And it seems I'm not alone. According to Harvard Medical School, "Gratitude helps people connect to something larger than themselves as individuals – whether to other people, nature, or a higher power." The author goes on to say, "In positive psychology research, gratitude is strongly and consistently associated with greater happiness. Gratitude helps people feel more positive emotions, relish good experiences, improve their health, deal with adversity, and build strong relationships."[35]

Some people express their gratitude with a daily gratitude journal. Others do a "buds and thorns" exercise each night around the dinner table, where they share the rosebuds of their day, the good moments, and the thorns of their day, the tough moments, and they end with asking each person to share what they're grateful for. Still others actually say blessings throughout the day to remind themselves to be grateful – from blessing their ability to wake up in the morning, to blessing their food before they eat, to saying a blessing at night before they go to bed.

In the Jewish tradition, we have hundreds of blessings to show gratitude. We even have one to say thanks after we use the restroom. It says, essentially: "Thank you God for creating

---

34. Greg Marcus, *The Spiritual Practice of Good Actions: Finding Balance through the Soul Traits of Mussar* (Woodbury, Minnesota: Llewellyn Publications, 2016), 8.

35. "Giving Thanks Can Make You Happier," *Harvard Health Publishing*, last modified June 17, 2020, https://www.health.harvard.edu/healthbeat/giving-thanks-can-make-you-happier.

us with many openings and hollow spaces, and thank you for making them work right, opening when they're supposed to and closing them when they're supposed to. I know that even if one of them would remain sealed, it would be impossible to survive."

Did you know that Judaism has a wonderful catchall blessing you can say just to recognize that being alive today, right now, at this moment is pretty darn cool? It's called the *shehekhiyanu* and simply says, "Thank you God for keeping me alive, sustaining me, and letting me reach this moment in time."

Naomi Levy has a beautiful book called *Talking to God*, in which she offers hundreds of wonderful, accessible prayers for everyday life, as well as for less common circumstances. For me, I try to end the day when I'm lying in bed thinking about three things I'm thankful for. It's a good way for me to end the day on a positive note, no matter how difficult or frustrating a day it was.

I'll add one last example of how I ensure that my own personal spirituality makes Jewish life meaningful and relevant for me today. In the Shema, the blessing we consider the "watchword" of our faith, we say, "God is One," and most interpret that to mean there is one God and not many gods like the polytheists believed. However, I interpret it to mean God is all things. God is *the One*.

Additionally, in the beginning of the prayer, when we say, "Hear, O Israel," I don't interpret that to mean, "Hey Jews, listen up – I have something important to tell you." Instead, I understand it as, "Hey Jews, listen up – listen to the world around you! Listen to the sounds of nature and the universe. *That* is God talking to you."

Ultimately, I believe in the importance of taking steps along the path. When it comes to spirituality, whatever you do, it's important to do something. Danny Gordis writes in *God Was Not in the Fire*, "Spiritual progress requires spiritual work. Judaism's unique spiritual gift is its amalgam of concrete ways of life that are designed to foster not only wandering and the wondering, but discovery as well."[36]

✡ ✡ ✡

I want to end this chapter coming back to a lesson I shared earlier. The Torah teaches us that when Moses gives the Torah to the People of Israel, they respond, "*Naaseh v'nishma*," which means, "We will do and we will hear."[37] This is interpreted to mean that sometimes we need to do things even if we don't yet understand why. And in the doing, the understanding will often come. It might come later, but it will come. The important thing is to do.

For me, Jewish Peoplehood includes all seven of these areas of TACHLIS. But for others, it may just be one or two. That's okay. I say, start there and see where it takes you. Ideally, you'll enjoy it, find meaning in it and will want to take on additional elements. But for starters, just pick one, and in the doing, you may just discover the meaning.

---

36. Gordis, *God Was Not in the Fire*, 73.
37. Exodus 24:7.

6

The Next Big Jewish Idea:
LEAP Year

In 1986, I was thirteen years old. I was into cool cars and '80s sitcoms. I went to a public junior high school and played soccer on a neighboring club team, the Upland Celtics, not the Claremont Stars where my classmates played. And I went to Hebrew school three days a week in another neighboring town which was home to the only Reform shul within a twenty-mile radius.

I had been going to Hebrew school for four years with the same dozen kids from the same five nearby towns. We were members of Temple Beth Israel, where the rabbi, Earl Kaplan (of blessed memory), had a gift for keeping the younger kids engaged with his puppet shows. Rabbi Kaplan was from Chicago and was a huge fan of the Chicago Bears. He had a poster of Ditka's 1985 team in his office with William "The Refrigerator" Perry, which I remember clearly because I spent a lot of time looking at it while I was in the rabbi's office. Not by choice.

My parents made me go to Hebrew school three times a week, and I was always getting into trouble. It seems that every other week I was being sent to the principal's office, or worse, Rabbi Kaplan's office, for acting out. But Rabbi Kaplan was a nice guy, and he was friends with my parents, so he took it easy on me. He knew I did not want to be stuck in a tiny classroom on a hot, sunny California afternoon with an Israeli lady speaking to me in a language I didn't understand after I had spent the entire day inside my regular school classroom and all I wanted to do was run around and play.

But this is what we did. We suffered through Hebrew school because our parents suffered through Hebrew school. And we did it to prepare for our bar mitzvah. This was – and for the most part still is – the culmination of the Jewish journey for non-Orthodox Jewish kids in America. This arduous rite of passage of going through Hebrew school is passed on from one Jewish generation to the next as if it were encoded in our DNA. But in the end, all thirteen-year-old Jewish kids are willing to put up with it because of that one word that Tevye sings so passionately: "Tradition!" Oh, and for some, the party and the presents are also a nice incentive.

The idea of the Jewish coming of age ceremony is actually beautiful. The marking of an important moment in our development, moving from childhood into adulthood, is one more way that Judaism has figured out how to mark time. Judaism really does life-cycle events well; it's actually a moment I believe should be marked by other communities, too. However, not counting a few exceptions at some very creative Jewish institutions in the US, the current system of going through Hebrew school for most non-Orthodox kids today is painful, archaic, and counter-productive.

The tragedy is that the bar or bat mitzvah should be the beginning of a young Jew's Jewish journey, not the culmination.

But by the time kids go through the three or four years of torture, they're done. What a missed opportunity!

First of all, instead of making kids miserable going through Hebrew school, the process should be more exciting, engaging, and meaningful, so these young Jews want to continue their learning and practicing of Judaism. So, what if we could inspire their Jewish journey rather than extinguish it? Don't we owe it to that next generation to come up with a new model?

The answer is yes, absolutely, of course! Which is why I'm not the first person to suggest this. In fact, when I Googled "making Hebrew school better," Google returned over forty-nine million hits! Okay, so what if part of the problem is that this is just the life of a thirteen-year-old? They are busy running in a million different directions – from sports practice to music rehearsals to art classes – and Hebrew school falls pretty low on the priority list unless it's a lot of fun.

Perhaps we need to extend out the pinnacle of one's Jewish education a few more years. Perhaps the b'nai mitzvah should be one step along a longer path and young Jews should instead hit an apex along their path to Jewish adulthood when they are eighteen years old.[1] Perhaps the Jewish community should strive to make this high point a collective experience when they are finishing high school and moving on to the next phase of their lives. Perhaps pushing out this peak moment a few more years will also allow the community to address a few other challenges as well.

---

1. Part of the beginning of this chapter is taken from an article I co-wrote with Nir Braudo from BINA for eJewishphilanthropy https://ejewishphilanthropy. com/a-jewish-leap-year-the-new-bnai-mitzvah/.

What challenges do I have in mind? Well, I can think of four more in particular...

First, as mentioned in chapter three, Diaspora Jews and Israeli Jews increasingly have less and less in common with each other. This is leading to a lack of understanding of Jewish Peoplehood as our binding ideal and, in some cases, open animosity toward the other. What if we could create real relationships between Israeli and Diaspora Jews, exposing them not just to each other's challenges, but also to one another's homes, traditions, practices, and so much of the other good stuff, too?

Another example of a challenge we face today is that many young Jews, especially American Jews, arrive on college campuses unprepared for the challenges they'll face – challenges to their Jewish identity, challenges to their relationship with Israel, as well as challenges of living independently and far from home. What if we could offer these young Diaspora Jews an opportunity to strengthen their Jewish identity before they go to college? What if we could offer them a longer on-ramp to independence as well?

Third, most Israelis still don't know there are many options for how to live Jewishly because they believe they must choose between a false dichotomy: either you are *chiloni* (secular) or *dati* (Orthodox). They don't know that a rich continuum exists between the two polar extremes because they haven't been exposed to it. So what if young Israelis, in that period just before they join the IDF, were exposed to the many different ways of doing Jewish that exist in the Diaspora just at that very moment when they are forming their own Jewish identities? What if they could form meaningful bonds with Jews of different backgrounds, religious practices, and beliefs in the most formative moment in their lives, and then take that back to Israel with them?

Finally, differences within the Jewish community are becoming so divisive that we are losing our sense of unity, forgetting the notion of looking out for one other and the basic tenet of *am echad* (Peoplehood). What if we could bring our young people together so they see beyond our different religious practices, our different political opinions, and our different cultural norms? What if we could transcend our differences and reignite the value of *kol Yisrael arevim zeh ba'zeh*, that all Jews are responsible for each other?

I believe we can address all these challenges by creating a new ritual in Jewish life, a new experience that marks another important milestone: high school graduation.

A New Rite of Passage for Another Milestone

Imagine a time in the near future when the new norm in Jewish life will be a transformative period between young Jews' graduation from high school and heading off to college or the Israeli army. Imagine if a gap year becomes part of the ethos of all Jews around the world.

Many Israeli Jews are doing this already, taking a gap year before they go on to do their army service through what's called a *mechina* program, but it's still not yet the norm. But imagine it becomes the norm for Israelis, and imagine it also becomes the norm for Diaspora Jews, who will spend a year together, doing national service, exploring their heritage, learning to create a Jewish life for themselves, engaged in Tikkun Olam, being exposed to other places in the Jewish world, and getting to know other Jewish eighteen-year-olds from around the globe in a real way.

Imagine a time when so many Israeli Jews are exposed to and inspired by Diaspora Judaism, that they bring back home a pluralistic and contemporary Judaism that replicates the inspiring Shabbat service of American Jewish summer camps, or Passover in the Desert by Wilderness Torah, or Jewish women's circles like At the Well, or the creative Torah reading of Rabbi Amichai Lau-Lavie's StorahTelling. When a critical mass emerges in Israel that fuels some of the budding alternatives to Orthodoxy, it could lead to a groundswell acceptance among Israelis to make non-Orthodox Jewish weddings, conversions, and funerals legal for Israeli Jews.

Taglit-Birthright has done important work to help Jewish millennials rethink their own relationship to Israel and their own Jewish identity. But ten days is not enough. At this important moment in a person's life, programming must include deeper encounters between Diaspora and Israeli Jews, serious and relevant Jewish textual study, as well as meaningful and sustainable opportunities for social action.

The Jewish Agency's *shlichim* (emissaries) and *shin-shinim* (also emissaries, but in this case the term is short for *shenat sherut*, meaning "year of service") programs that send Israelis to the Diaspora are wonderful, but they're also not enough. It's one thing to work in a Jewish summer camp, a JCC, or a Jewish day school, but these Israelis are only seeing a tiny slice of Diaspora Judaism and are not really being exposed to the vast mosaic of Jewish life. (They're not even seeing the bulk of American Jewish life, much less Jewish life in the rest of the world.) The role of the *shaliach* (the singular of *shlichim*) – which can be understood from its very literal definition of "messenger" – needs to be updated. The notion that their job is to be emissaries of Israel, to bring a bit of Israeli culture and society to the Diaspora, is an inspired idea, but we now know it needs to be a two-way street; just as Jews around the world can learn so much about Israel from *shlichim*, Israeli Jews have so much to learn about Judaism from the diversity and richness that world Jewry has to offer.

The solution to these challenges is to change the paradigm in the Jewish community so that a new conviction emerges that the apex of a young person's Jewish journey is no longer their b'nai mitzvah, but a gap year experience between high school and college, or high school and the army – though not a gap year, but a Jewish LEAP Year.

The Jewish LEAP Year

LEAP is an acronym that stands for Learning, Experience, Action, and Peoplehood. The Jewish LEAP year is a new take on the gap year experience, and it reflects the belief that one's Jewish identity – indeed, one's identity as a whole – is incomparably affected by immersive experiences as a teenager. The Jewish LEAP year affirms the common understanding that a meaningful Jewish life is comprised of Jewish literacy, a meaningful exchange between different types of Jews, participation in social justice activities, and deep friendships. The Jewish LEAP year creates paths toward each of these elements, and in doing so, cultivates Jewish lives that can be part of architecting a new Jewish future.

Three core principles make the Jewish LEAP year distinct from other gap year experiences:

1. Half the participants will be Israeli and half will be from the Diaspora.

2. The year will be split so part of the time is spent in Israel, part in America, and part in another part of the world, i.e., Europe or Latin America.

3. The curriculum will be based on the four key elements that are in the name: Learning, Experience, Action and Peoplehood.

A typical week on a LEAP Year could include:

- Learning both traditional and modern Jewish texts with lectures, classes, and traditional *hevruta* study.[2]
- Social action Tikkun Olam projects and local volunteering with Jewish organizations that cover a vast array of topics from helping the hungry and homeless to assisting refugees to taking care of the environment to building homes to assisting in disaster spots.
- Creating meaningful Jewish rituals for the group, including their own way of celebrating Shabbat as well as reimagining upcoming Jewish holidays
- Touring local Jewish sites, encountering the local community, and engaging in local cultural experiences
- Group bonding and reflection aimed at fostering individual Jewish identity

On the one hand, the JCC system could be well-positioned to pull this off, as there is a global network of JCCs. So, for example, participants could spend three to four months based at a JCC in Israel through the Israel Association of Community

---

2. *Chevruta* study means two people studying a traditional text in a pair.

Centers, then another three to four months at a JCC in the US arranged through the JCC Association of North America, then another three to four months at a JCC in another country, arranged by the JCC Global network.

On the other hand, JCCs are not in the gap year business while other organizations are. So, it may make more sense to collaborate and partner with them, encouraging them to add some LEAP elements to their already existing programs, namely the mingling of Israeli and Diaspora Jews and hosting part of the year in different countries. This is indeed what the OFJCC and BINA are doing. We are partnering to prototype a LEAP Year program in the summer of 2021 and 2022. If all goes well, this could be a model to share with other providers, since there are indeed many great gap year programs out there.

Jewish American organizations like Young Judaea, Ramah, Kivunim, and Tivnu host wonderful gap years, while Israeli programs exist for Diaspora Jews as well, including BINA, Ein Prat, and The Shalom Hartman Institute. (For those interested, the organization Masa is an important central address for listing the gap years that exist today.) Again, the key in my mind, however, is the interchange between Israeli and Diaspora Jews, and spending significant time in different locations. This will help make the idea of a year between high school and college (or the army) normative in the minds of Jewish parents.

In David Brooks' book *The Second Mountain*, he calls for a renewal of the village spirit that existed once when people looked out for each other, helped each other, and came together. He calls for rebirthing the communal notion of coming together for each other, for a common cause by building something together in the formative years in life. He says the following:

> When people come together to build something, they make implied promises to one another. They promise to work things out. They promise to do their fair share or more of the work. They promise to follow through on the intention to build something new.... Just as a couple make vows to each other at a wedding ceremony, I sometimes think that communities should organize a village compact ceremony.... A modern ceremony could involve a group of people swearing loyalty to one another, specifying what sorts of projects they are willing to take, what price they are willing to pay. A modern ceremony could have initiation rites, rituals of mutual belonging, the retelling of the community story, symbols that signify common membership, and a sacred meeting spot, where people across generations can make their vows. Then of course there'd be a party.[3]

The LEAP Year could be created around these same ideas: building something together, committing to one another, rituals of belonging, retelling the Jewish story, making places sacred, and of course partying together.

✡   ✡   ✡

---

3.   David Brooks, *The Second Mountain: The Quest for a Moral Life* (New York: Random House, 2019), 287–88.

I believe we need a new vision for the Jewish future – one that creates a new model for living a meaningful Jewish life in the twenty-first century and one that creates a new paradigm for relations between Israel and world Jewry. And I believe it involves taking a leap over the chasm of the old ways to the new.

There is a midrash associated with the Exodus story that is not in the Bible. According to the Torah, when Moses led the Israelites out of slavery and he reached the shores of the Red Sea, they got stuck. The people looked forward and saw nothing but a vast sea they couldn't cross, and they panicked. They looked backward and saw the most terrifying army of the time, Pharaoh's horses and chariots, barreling down upon them. They rose up in fear and shouted to Moses, "Is it because there are no graves in Egypt that you have taken us to die in the desert?... You should have left us alone to serve the Egyptians rather than die here in the desert!"[4]

Meanwhile, Moses instructs the people to not be afraid and to trust God, but he himself doesn't know what to do. He also panics. He calls out to God for help, and God says, "Why do you call out to me? Raise up your staff over the water and split the sea."[5]

And while Moses is working up his courage to do something, there is this man who realizes talk is cheap and action must be taken. This man, Nachshon, gets down to business and he leaps into the Red Sea. He takes the leap! I like to think of it as a leap of faith mixed with his need to get down to *tachlis* and just finally do something!

It was Nahshon's leap that helped part the Red Sea and

---

4.   Exodus 14:11–12.
5.   Exodus 14:15–16.

gave the rest of the Israelites the faith to follow him, and that's ultimately what saved them.

Just as Nahshon took a leap into the Red Sea, so too must we take a leap.

We must leap over the old apex of the Jewish journey to create a new apex.

We must leap over those "lost" years between the bar or bat mitzvah and the end of high school to create a new transformative Jewish experience.

We must leap over the chasm between Israeli Jewry and Diaspora Jewry to create new bridges and weave together our future.

I hope you join me in taking the LEAP together.

Epilogue

When I was eight years old and my brother Gabe was five, we were visited by one of my father's close friends, Uncle Gary. He wasn't an uncle, but we called many of my dad's close buddies "Uncle." I'm not sure why some deserved that moniker and others didn't, but alas, another foolish inconsistency.

In any case, Uncle Gary was well off. He drove a vintage Jaguar XKE, he was the first person I knew to own a large-screen TV, and he had all the newest gadgets and toys. Granted this was the early '80s, but we were sill awed by our ability to play Space Invaders on a ginormous screen in his living room.

Just before my family was about to move from Atlanta, Georgia, to Southern California, Uncle Gary came over for a farewell visit. He took me and Gabe to a giant toy store and told us to pick anything we wanted and he'd buy it for us.

Now I don't remember if this was just a local mom-and-pop store or a giant Toys R Us, but it felt huge. Dare I say, it even felt too big. Yes, I know that sounds crazy – how could any toy store be too big for a couple of young boys? But it really was just too big.

I remember vividly what happened next: I was so overwhelmed that I ended up sitting in the middle of the store crying because I couldn't make up my mind. There were just too many wonderful toys to choose from. I had no limits. I could choose anything. Nothing was too big or too expensive. Uncle Gary gave us zero limitations. He said, "Choose whatever you want."

In the end, I walked away with a 90-cent necklace. No joke. My mother verifies this story and to this day, she shakes her head laughing. My mom has always been open-minded, non-judgmental, and filled with love for me and my brother. Like most Jewish mothers, she thinks her sons can do no wrong. But I actually think she looks back on that moment and believes I totally blew it.

The lesson for me is that it's possible to have too many choices. You can actually have too much freedom. Sometimes limitations are a good thing. Sometimes guard rails actually give us more flexibility. When we're set off with no rules, no direction and the only guidance is, "Go anywhere you want," it can be paralyzing – or if not paralyzing, at least a waste of vital energy just getting started.

In the book *The Cloister Walk*, Kathleen Norris says one of the hallmarks of her time spent with Benedictine monks was noticing that energy could be put toward important decisions instead of the silly, inconsequential ones. She gives the example of breakfast choices, quoting a monk who "was troubled by the growing number of cereals made available for breakfast in his community. 'How many kinds of cereals do we need,' he asked, 'in order to meet genuine health needs without falling into thoughtless consumerism?'"[6]

By providing only one cereal in the monastery, Norris did not have the freedom to choose other options for breakfast. But instead of this limiting her, she found it gave her a new freedom from having to choose. It gave her a freedom of simplicity. It gave her a freedom to expend her energy on more important choices.

It makes me think of how famous tech titans Steve Jobs

---

6.   Kathleen Norris, *The Cloister Walk* (New York: Riverhead Books, 1987), 15.

and Mark Zuckerberg always wore a variation of the same outfit to work every day. An article in *Forbes* claimed that at least for some of these geniuses who wore the same work uniform daily, it was an efficient way to not "waste brainpower" on an unimportant decision.[7]

For me, Judaism serves the same purpose. By setting me off on a path with a direction and by giving me some basic guardrails, I have a road map. It doesn't mean I must take a predetermined path. It doesn't mean I have to end up at a set destination. And it doesn't mean the journey will be without detours.

On the contrary, I will still make countless decisions along the road. There will still be moments of struggle, times when I'm unsure what to do next, times when I wrestle with God. And of course, there will be times when I wonder if I took a wrong turn. I will be filled with self-doubt. I will be cursed with regret. But there will also be moments of grace and transcendence. That is the nature of free will.

Yochi Brandes captures this brilliantly in her novel *The Orchard* when, toward the end of the book, Rabbi Akiva is distraught and overcome with regret and confesses, "I wanted to teach the nation of Israel that our fate is in our own hands. We conduct our own lives and determine our own future. Everything is foreseen, yet free will is given."[8]

This contradiction is at the heart of what it means to do

7.   Jacquelyn Smith, "Steve Jobs Always Dressed Exactly the Same. Here's Who Else Does," *Forbes*, October 5, 2012, https://www.forbes.com/sites/jacquelynsmith/2012/10/05/steve-jobs-always-dressed-exactly-the-same-heres-who-else-does/

8.   Yochi Brandes, *The Orchard* (Jerusalem: Gefen Publishing House, 2017), 373.

Jewish. We must be able to hold in our hands at the same time the idea that our destiny as a people is already determined, and yet every decision is ours to make as individuals. All of existence is prewritten, while every letter is ours to write. We must choose what road to take even though that choice is foreseen. That is how we are partners with God in creation. That is how we are part of the Jewish story.

The Israeli philosopher Micah Goodman makes the case in his book *The Wondering Jew* that engaging in this very discussion is what keeps the Jewish People together; the engagement is the vital step along the path. He writes, "If faith is not what connects one hundred generations of Jews, what does? The answer: Judaism is the Jews' ongoing conversation. The conversation about Judaism *is* Judaism. The way Jews become connected to Judaism is by joining the Jewish conversation. Even those who disagree with the content of the tradition can still be a part of the tradition, because a disagreement with previous generations is still a conversation with them."[9]

That is the point of this book – to encourage you to engage in the conversation, join the journey, take the first step, or your *next* step. It doesn't matter where you are along the path, just travel with us. Be part of the adventure. Learn. Listen. Talk. Argue. Do. And if you do, it just might make all the difference in giving your life meaning, purpose, and joy.

Now, who's ready to take that next step?

---

9. Micah Goodman, *The Wondering Jew: Israel and the Search for Jewish Identity*, (New Haven: Yale University Press, 2020), 91.

References

Books referenced in *Why Do Jewish?* which I recommend for **Deeper Thinking** on the subjects covered:

Torah

Talmud

Brandes, Yochi. *The Orchard.* Jerusalem: Gefen Publishing House, 2017.

Bronfman, Edgar M. *Why Be Jewish?: A Testament.* New York: Twelve, 2016.

Brooks, David. *The Second Mountain: The Quest for a Moral Life.* New York: Random House, 2019.

Fuchs, Camil, and Shmuel Rosner. *#IsraeliJudaism: Portrait of a Cultural Revolution.* Jerusalem: The Jewish People Policy Institute, 2019.

Goldstein, Niles. *Gonzo Judaism: A Bold Path for Renewing an Ancient Faith.* Trumpeter, 2010.

Goodman, Micah. *The Wondering Jew: Israel and the Search for Jewish Identity.* New Haven: Yale University Press, 2020.

Gordis, Daniel. *We Stand Divided: The Rift between American Jews and Israel.* New York: Ecco, 2019.

———. *God Was Not in the Fire: The Search for Spiritual Judaism.* New York: Scribner, 1995.

Green, Arthur. *Judaism's 10 Best Ideas: A Brief Guide for Seekers.* Woodstock, VT: Jewish Lights, 2014.

———. *Radical Judaism: Rethinking God and Tradition.* New Haven: Yale University Press, 2010.

Heschel, Abraham Joshua. *The Sabbath.* New York: Farrar, Straus, and Giroux, 1951.

―――. *God in Search of Man*. New York: Farrar, Straus, and Giroux, 1976.

Hurwitz, Sarah. *Here All Along: Finding Meaning, Spirituality, and Deeper Connection to Life – in Judaism (After Finally Choosing to Look There)*. New York: Random House, 2019.

Infeld, Avraham. *A Passion for a People: Lessons from the Life of a Jewish Educator*. Jerusalem: Melitz, 2017.

Kaplan, Mordecai. *Judaism as a Civilization: Toward the Reconstruction of American-Jewish Life*. New York: Shocken Books, 1967.

Kaunfer, Elie. *Empowered Judaism: What Independent Minyanim Can Teach Us About Building Vibrant Jewish Communities*. Woodstock, VT: Jewish Lights, 2010.

Keinan, Tal. *God Is in the Crowd: Twenty-First Century Judaism*. New York: Spiegel & Grau, 2018.

Kornbluth, Doron. *Why Be Jewish? Knowledge and Inspiration for Jews of Today*. Beit Shemesh: Mosaica Press, 2011.

Kushner, Harold S. *When Bad Things Happen to Good People*. New York: Anchor Books, 2004.

Levy, Naomi. *Talking to God: Personal Prayers for Times of Joy, Sadness, Struggle, and Celebration*. New York: Knopf, 2002.

Lew, Alan. *This Is Real and You Are Completely Unprepared*. New York: Little, Brown, and Co., 2003.

Magid, Shaul. *American Post-Judaism: Identity and Renewal in a Postethnic Society*. Bloomington, IN: Indiana University Press, 2013.

Marcus, Greg. *The Spiritual Practice of Good Actions*. Woodbury, Minnesota: Llewellyn Publications, 2016.

Mnookin, Robert. *The Jewish American Paradox: Embracing Choice in a Changing World*. New York: PublicAffairs, 2018.

Norris, Kathleen. *The Cloister Walk*. New York: Riverhead Books, 1987.

Ochs, Vanessa. *Inventing Jewish Ritual*. Philadelphia: The Jewish Publication Society, 2007.

Pogrebin, Abigail. *My Year of Living Jewishly: 18 Holidays, One Wondering Jew*. Bedford, NY: Fig Tree Books, 2017.

Rushkoff, Douglas. *Nothing Sacred: The Truth About Judaism*. New York: Crown Publishers, 2003.

Sacks, Jonathan. *A Letter in the Scroll*. New York: The Free Press, 2000.

———. *Celebrating Life*. New York: Bloomsbury USA, 2019.

———. *Lessons in Leadership: A Weekly Reading of the Jewish Bible*. Jerusalem: Maggid Books, 2015.

Sharansky, Natan, and Gil Troy. *Never Alone: Prison, Politics, and My People*. New York: Hachette Book Group, 2020.

Shlain, Tiffany. *24/6: The Power of Unplugging One Day a Week*. New York: Gallery Books, 2019.

Tolle, Eckart. *Practicing the Power of Now*. Novato, CA: New World Library, 1999.

Tzu, Lao. *Tao Te Ching*. Translated by Stephen Addiss and Stanley Lombardo. Indianapolis: Hackett Publishing Company, 1993.

Vogl, Charles. *The Art of Community: Seven Principles for Belonging*. Oakland, CA: Berrett-Koehler Publishers, 2016.

Wolpe, David J. *Why Be Jewish?* New York: Owl Books, 1995.

Organizations referenced in *Why Do Jewish?* that I recommend for **Further Doing** on various subjects:

o   18Doors – www.18doors.org
o   929 – https://929.org.il
o   92Y – www.92Y.org
o   AIPAC – www.aipac.org
o   At the Well – www.atthewellproject.com
o   BBYO – https://bbyo.org
o   Be'chol Lashon – www.globaljews.org
o   BimBam – www.bimbam.com
o   BINA – www.bina.org.il
o   Burning Man – www.burningman.org
o   Center for Jewish Peoplehood Education – www.jpeoplehood.org
o   Chabad – www.chabad.org
o   Days United – www.daysunited.com
o   Ein Prat – www.ein-prat.com
o   ERAN – https://en.eran.org.il
o   Gideon Hausner Jewish Day School – https://hausner.school
o   HaMaqom – https://hmqm.org
o   HIAS – www.hias.org
o   Honeymoon Israel – www.honeymoonisrael.org
o   Israel Association of Community Centers – https://matnasim.org
o   JCC Global – www.jccglobal.org
o   JCC Greater Boston – www.bostonjcc.org
o   JCC Maccabi Games – www.jccmaccabigames.org
o   Jewish Agency – www.jewishagency.org
o   Jewish Community Center Association of North America – www.jcca.org
o   Jewish Community Federation of San Francisco – www.jewishfed.org
o   Jewish Education Project – www.jewishedproject.org
o   Jewish Funders' Network – www.jfunders.org

o   Jewish Initiative for Animals – www.jewishinitiativeforanimals.org

o   Jewish Studio Project – www.jewishstudioproject.org

o   Jews of Color Initiative – www.jewsofcolorinitiative.org

o   Judaism Unbound – www.judaismunbound.com

o   Kivunim – www.kivunim.org

o   Lab/Shul – https://labshul.org

o   Marlene Meyerson JCC of Manhattan – www.mmjccm.org

o   Masa Israel – www.masaisrael.org

o   Moishe House – www.moishehouse.org

o   One Table – www.onetable.org

o   OpenDor Media – www.opendormedia.org

o   Oshman Family JCC – www.paloaltojcc.org

o   Pardes – www.pardes.org.il

o   PJ Library – https://pjlibrary.org

o   Ramah – www.ramah.org.il

o   REBOOT – www.rebooters.net

o   Sefaria – www.sefaria.org

o   Shalom Hartman Institute – www.hartman.org.il

o   SlingShot – www.slingshotfund.org

o   Svara – www.svara.org

o   Tivnu – https://tivnu.org

o   UpStart – www.upstartlab.org

o   URJ – www.urj.org

o   Wilderness Torah – www.wildernesstorah.org

o   Young Judaea – www.youngjudaea.org

o   Z3 Project – www.z3project.org

Index

About the Author

Zack Bodner is a seeker, writer, storyteller, community organizer, and above all else, a doer. While serving as the CEO of the Oshman Family Jewish Community Center, he oversaw the creation of the Center for Social Impact, the Taube Center for Jewish Peoplehood, and the Z3 Project, a global effort to reimagine Diaspora-Israel relations.

Before joining the JCC, Zack served for fourteen years as the Pacific Northwest Regional Director of AIPAC. Zack holds a master's degree in philosophy of religion and theology from Claremont Graduate University and a bachelor's degree from Yale University. Additionally, he studied at Hebrew University in Jerusalem, Ohr Somayach yeshiva, and Stanford Graduate School of Business.

Zack is an accomplished speaker, including as a MOTH storyteller and TEDx presenter. He is a member of YPO, participated in the Executive Leadership Seminar at the Aspen Institute, and is on the Advisory Board of the Taube Center for Jewish Studies at Stanford University.

Zack lives in Silicon Valley with his wife and three children.